Transition to Adulthood

TRANSITION TO ADULTHOOD

for

Young People with Severe Learning Difficulties

Matthew Griffiths

David Fulton Publishers

London

David Fulton Publishers Ltd
2 Barbon Close, London WC1N 3JX

First published in Great Britain by
David Fulton Publishers 1994

Copyright © Matthew Griffiths

British Library Cataloguing in Publication Data

A catalogue record for this book is available from the British Library

ISBN 1-85346-251-9   LC 94228746

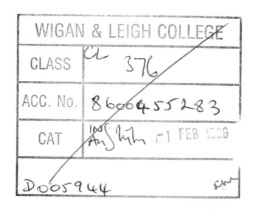
Designed by Almac Ltd., London
Typeset by ROM Data Corporation Ltd, Falmouth
Printed in Great Britain by the Cromwell Press, Melksham

Contents

CHAPTER 1

THE ADOLESCENT TRANSITION

The right of people with disabilities to full adult status is increasingly acknowledged.

As people with severe learning difficulties are perceived as potential adults, their teenage years become more significant. Adulthood is not attainable without an adolescent transition; typically this takes place in the teens and early twenties.

Adult status is easy to recognise but difficult to define, but in any society it is accorded to those who meet that particular society's criteria for adulthood. These criteria are centred on physical maturity, personal autonomy, productive activity and separation from parents, as individuals develop the capacity to take responsibility for themselves and others. This change in status and identity is a major transition.

In small and technologically unsophisticated societies, childhood can end relatively abruptly and transition to adulthood is brief. The onset of puberty and various social rituals can give immediate access to full adult status in every aspect of the individual's life.

In complex industrialised societies there are many more aspects of adulthood, many different roles to be performed and a wide variety of skills to be acquired. Transition to adulthood is protracted and complex and the process does not encompass all aspects of the young person's life at the same time. Adulthood is not recognised as a single event evident to everyone, instead a number of small changes in status and recognitions of the progress towards adult status take place over a number of years.

Adolescence is the period when the transitions take place which will take the young person from childhood to adulthood and into full adult status. Each transitional change brings with it both new opportunities and new responsibilities.

The physical changes of puberty, which usually begin in the early teens, mark the beginning of the process. The young person is reaching physical maturity and is now seen as moving towards adult status. However, depending on a number of factors, including culture and social class, adult status does not become a reality until between four to ten years after puberty. Physical adulthood does not confer adult status until the adolescent transition is completed.

A major marker of transition for many young people is the end of compulsory schooling at the age of sixteen. ~ 1954?

Traditionally this meant the beginning of employment and a major shift towards adult status for the young person. Instead of being dependent members of the family, for whom everything was provided by others, young people would become capable of providing for themselves. They could even begin to contribute to the family income instead of being supported by it. Changes in the labour market however mean that this direct form of transition to adult status is now made by comparatively few school-leavers.

Most young people who would have entered employment on leaving school, now move on to a vocational or pre-vocational course in further education or into Youth Training before entering full employment. Transition is delayed and young people remain financially dependent on their parents for longer than in the past.

Confusingly however, other recognitions of adult status are given to sixteen and seventeen year olds before they reach legal adulthood at eighteen. These include:

- the right to have sexual intercourse
- the right to marry
- the right to learn to drive
- the right to join the armed forces.

At eighteen a young person is legally an adult and has access to all the rights, experiences and obligations of adulthood.

Legal adulthood and physical maturity are the basis for adult status. However, most eighteen year olds would not be regarded as having full adult status. Most young people in the UK are probably in their early twenties before they are accorded full adult status by other adults or think of themselves as fully adult despite, for example, legal recognition of their adulthood.

Adult status is, however, accorded to young people who marry during their teens and to young mothers. They have taken on that responsibility to, and for, others, which is central to adult status. The shift of responsibility which is central to the transition is illustrated below, and young people with adult responsibilities are accorded that status even though they may not fulfil other criteria such as age, experience or personal autonomy.

The shift of responsibility from childhood to full adult status

Phase	Level of responsibility
Childhood	Others are responsible for making every provision for the child. *Childhood exemption* (Gagnon 1977) also ensures that everything a child does is viewed in a way which protects it from responsibility. Children are seen as not understanding the consequences of their actions. For example, a child under the age of ten cannot be charged with a criminal offence.
Late childhood/ early adolescence	Others are still totally responsible for making all provisions. The child is however, learning to take more responsibility for itself. 'Childhood exemption' is beginning to fall away and the child is increasingly judged by, and held accountable for, its own actions.
Mid to late adolescence	Although others may still be providing totally or in part for the young person, he/she is taking considerable responsibility for his/her own life and is learning to, or beginning to, provide for him/herself. 'Childhood exemption' has almost fully lapsed in many areas of life.
Early adulthood	Full responsibility for oneself. Managing one's own affairs, being instrumental in decision-making about one's own life. Individual now accountable for his/her own actions and

their consequences, although some allowances are still made for youth and inexperience.

| Full adult status | Responsibility for oneself and others, either as part of a family or as part of society. |

The aim of the transitional process can be divided into broad areas of life. (*Young people with Handicaps: The Road to Adulthood* OECD/CERI 1986).

These are:

– *personal autonomy* (full responsibility for one's own life)
– *productive activity* (economic self-sufficiency)
– *social interaction and community participation* (taking an adult role in society)
– *roles within the family* (being a non-dependent son or daughter, a spouse or a parent).

In each of these areas, a vital indicator of the successful achievement of 'adulthood' is the range of choices available to the individual, rather than any one particular choice or pattern of choices.

Most of these aspects of adult status are to some extent earned. They depend on:

– The individual having some skills.
– Other people acknowledging the individual's rights to deploy these skills and take on responsibility for decisions, productive work and new social and family roles.

Traditionally both of these have proved difficult for people with learning disabilities, particularly where they are very severe. Adults with severe learning disabilities may have difficulty in achieving adult status because:

– The disability itself precludes their achieving the level of competence generally regarded as necessary for adult status.

– They do not have access to the learning experiences which would enable them to develop greater competence.
– They have potential or actual competence, but their right to use it is not recognised by other people.

Young people and adults with severe learning difficulties are frequently handicapped in all three areas.

Parents and professionals can minimise the handicap by ensuring that young people:

- have as many skills as possible; particularly skills which will enable them to make the transition to adulthood.
- have access to learning opportunities which will enable them to develop new skills and maintain those already learned.
- have their rights to use skills acknowledged.

For example:

Can a young person choose the clothes he or she wishes to wear? (This includes both ability and opportunity).

Does he or she have as many opportunities as possible to make choices of clothes?

Are differences in weather, occasion and fashion pointed out and discussed simply and frequently?

Is attention drawn (discreetly, of course) to what other people are wearing and why?

Finally and possibly most problematically, is the young person actually allowed the right to make a real choice about both the purchasing and day to day selection of clothing?

The extent to which individual young people can develop skills will, of course, depend on innate ability, the cause of severe learning difficulties, motivation, experience and opportunity.

It is becoming increasingly clear however, that we underestimate the abilities and potential of people with severe learning difficulties. Our own lack of confidence in their abilities is often an even greater handicap than their innate lack of ability to develop and use skills.

This book is aimed at professionals in the field of education and it focuses on the role they can play in facilitating the achievement of adult status by people with severe learning difficulties.

Each phase of learning - school, further education, vocational training and the move into employment is considered separately because each has a specific role to play.

Other aspects of learning, such as self advocacy and the changing role of parents are vital to a successful transition to adult status and so they are considered in some detail.

The final chapters of the book concentrate on interagency collaboration because of the importance of a properly developed network of support for transition and on the mechanisms for an audit by which you can judge how effectively the provision you are making contributes to a successful adolescent transition.

The goals of adolescence are those which will enable the young person to successfully gain adult status.

Physical Maturity

If as adults, young people are to reproduce and take on a range of roles within the family, they must achieve physical maturity.

Cognitive Maturity

Again, if young people are to become workers, parents, voters or to take on any of the other adult roles in society, they must understand as much as possible about the world in which they live and have as mature as possible a view of it. Understanding continues to develop, of course, throughout adult life.

Emotional Maturity

Emotional maturity, like cognitive maturity, is not a fixed condition which is established in a phase of one's life, but the adolescent years are important in establishing the basis of an adult emotional maturity.

Older adolescents and young adults are capable of sexual relationships and are permitted by legislation and social custom to have them. It is therefore, desirable to have alongside the physical maturity and the social permission, the emotional level of development which enables them to understand responsibility towards another person, an empathy with their needs and feelings, a capacity for tenderness and the ability to give and receive affection.

It is also important, once young people have the physical maturity and the social permission to create children, that they are able to take on the emotional responsibilities and enjoy the emotional satisfactions of parents.

As the circle is completed, young people who become parents must be able to allow their children to be physically and emotionally dependent on them, just as they, before the beginning of the adolescent development, were dependent on their own parents.

An Individual Identity

Adolescence is the period during which, more than at any other time in our lives, we establish our own identity.

Ideas and attitudes about an individual's own identity have of course been evolving since earliest childhood. Young children begin by knowing their own names, their family, their sex, age and address. They establish the groups to which they belong and their own uniqueness within those groups.

Adolescence is a time for beginning to come to terms with one's own strength and weaknesses and to fashion a fulfilling life for the future in which so many different patterns exist for personal autonomy, productive activity, participation in the community and roles within the family.

Emancipation from Parents and Childhood

One of the goals for adolescence, as part of the development of emotional maturity and an adult identity, is the outgrowing of dependence on parents. This can involve a struggle which can be mixed with rebellion. Many parents mourn the passing of childhood and try to retain the dependence of their adolescent sons and daughters. Parents and adolescents frequently disagree about the levels of competence and capacity for independence and autonomy which a young person has reached.

When young people manage to emancipate themselves from their parents and their childhood role they are capable of directing their own lives without continuing to need, or either, to depend on their parents or defy them.

Adolescent transitions are seldom easy for any young people. The transition for a young person with severe learning difficulties can be even more difficult. It can even be prevented altogether so that men and women with severe learning difficulties remain frozen in childhood well into their adult years and possibly throughout their lives.

The next chapter looks specifically at adolescence for young people with severe learning difficulties within the framework of adolescent transition for all.

CHAPTER 2

SEVERE LEARNING DISABILITIES

The impact of a cognitive impairment on children and young people.

Chapter 1 described the process of adolescent transition as it applies to all young people. Adolescence was identified as a difficult time for every young person and possibly an insurmountable barrier for a young person with severe learning difficulties, both because of the disability itself and because of the impact which a disability has on the ways an individual is perceived and treated in every aspect of his or her life.

In the U.K. 'learning disability' (previously known as 'mental handicap' is officially defined as 'a state of arrested or incomplete development of mind that includes significant impairment of intelligence and social functioning', (Mental Health Act 1983).

In educational legislation the term ' "special educational needs" is used to denote someone who has a learning difficulty which requires special educational provision to be made for him'. (Education Act 1981, as amended by the Education Act 1993).

A child with a learning difficulty is one who has:

a significantly greater difficulty in learning than the majority of children of that age, or has a disability which either prevents or hinders him from making use of educational facilities of a kind generally provided in schools, within the area of the local authority concerned, for children of that age.

(Education Act 1981)

The Further and Higher Education Act of 1992 extends this definition into late adolescence and young adulthood and so it is applicable to young people who have left school.

Young people with learning disabilities, as defined by the Mental Health Act 1983 are a sub-group of young people with learning difficulties in educational terms. The terms are however, often used interchangeably.

'Learning difficulties' or *'learning disabilities'* are therefore currently acceptable terms for a range of disabilities which are actually disabilities of understanding or are a cognitive impairment. The causes of cognitive impairment are many and varied, few are well understood and many not understood at all. Impairment may result from damage to, or a malformation of, the brain or nervous system, before, during or after birth or during childhood. Whatever the cause of a cognitive impairment, it means that the individual will experience some degree of difficulty with:

– making sense of the world;
– feeling secure and safe in the world;
– predicting and understanding cause and effect;
– conceptualising and generalising;
– symbols and symbolic representation.

These are the core elements of learning disability. The degree of difficulty will differ, not only because of different degrees of impairment but because individuals have different personalities, life experiences and opportunities for learning.

All people who have learning disability find it very hard to understand the world in which they find themselves. Because they find their world difficult to understand, they have considerable problems with operating effectively in it.

These difficulties present fewest problems in babyhood and early childhood, when all babies and children are struggling to begin to understand the world and form concepts such as the permanence of objects (things remaining in existence even when they are out of sight); cause and effect and such concepts as communication and language; time and space and the cultural norms of behaviour.

As children grow older and the majority master the concepts which will allow them to take increasing control over their own lives, children with severe learning disabilities remain at a disadvantage in major ways :

– the nature and extent of their actual disability;
– the perception that they are children who have disabilities and that they therefore need to be treated in ways which are significantly different from those which apply to other children.

The nature and extent of the disability

There are real problems in truly understanding what it is like to have learning disabilities. People who have learning disabilities cannot, because of the very nature of the disability, conceptualise their difficulties or explain what it is like to have a very tenuous, partial, or fragmented understanding.

Sometimes, in disability awareness training events, a range of disabilities are simulated to try and provide some insight into what it is like to operate as an individual with a particular disability. For example:

- simulating a visual disability by using blindfolds or spectacles which give the effect of a range of specific problems;
- providing the effect of deafness or hearing impairment by using wax plugs, ear muffs or headphones which distance or relay noises similar to tinnitus;
- being confined to a wheelchair or having limbs immobilised by splints to simulate aspects of physical disability.

A cognitive impairment or disability of understanding is sometimes simulated, in this kind of exercise, by asking participants to copy strange hieroglyphics which apparently have meaning to the facilitator or by asking the participants to imagine themselves in a foreign country where they do not understand the spoken or written language, the currency, the social behaviour, or the geography.

Learning disabilities have a much deeper and more profound impact than anything that this kind of exercise can touch on.

The analogy of the foreign country in which the individual is lost, trying to work out some rules and some means of communicating with others, is not really useful because the person with significant global learning disabilities has major difficulties understanding the underlying concepts of the world, not just the particular ways in which these concepts are manifested in a particular country or society. For example:

- People with severe learning disabilities have difficulties with the formulation of ideas, particularly abstract ideas and with the transcription of these ideas firstly into words and then into writing, the symbolic representation of words.

- A foreigner who does not understand the particular language being spoken and written around him, does not have difficulties with the concept of language. He knows that language conveys meaning, even if he does not know what the meaning is.

Understanding, once gained, is usually irreversible. It is almost impossible to suspend understanding and it is therefore almost impossible to feel what it is like not to understand the basic ways the world operates.

Young people with severe learning disabilities find it hard to understand those basic ways in which the world operates and those who work with them often misunderstand the degree and extent of this lack of understanding. This is because many young people have learned a range of skills and strategies which enable them to cope with their world and the demands it makes upon them.

These skills and strategies often work very well throughout childhood and have traditionally worked well enough for the kinds of adult lives which people with severe learning disabilities have led. They are rooted in incomprehension and difficulty with understanding what is expected and often consist of:

Being passive.	Doing nothing unless specifically told to do it. This means that new things are not tried out and so there are few opportunities for teachers or others to see that a set of skills is actually an isolated raft in a sea of non-understanding or mis-understanding.
Waiting until shown.	If you are unsure what to do it is safest to wait until someone gives you an example. This is a variation of the advice given to people who don't know how to eat an unusual food, or are unsure which cutlery to use. - Don't do anything until you see what other people are doing.

Special schools for children with severe learning difficulties and anyone involved in the upbringing of the children can unwittingly collude with the establishment of these strategies and indeed can actively encourage them in a bid to make children acceptable and over-conformist to compensate for the perceived disadvantages of disability.

The passivity and conformity which are initially brought about by incomprehension are therefore extended and developed by the way in which the children and young people are educated and socialised.

Children are often praised for 'being good', which often means being passive, not challenging, questioning or taking risks, not questioning, asserting or disagreeing.

Given that most children and young people with severe learning disabilities, because of their incomprehension and insecurity in the world, are likely to be more passive and less disposed to experiment than most youngsters this style of socialisation is likely to succeed because it fits into an existing pre-disposition.

The perceptions of others are therefore a major factor in either minimising or maximising the handicapping effect of the intrinsic cognitive impairment.

Being perceived as a person with a learning difficulty is likely to influence the behaviour of others in a range of fundamental ways. Because people have a learning disability, they are likely to:

- be talked to less;
- have fewer explanations given to them;
- be precluded from taking part in activities which enable their peers to make more sense of the world and develop skills;
- be encouraged to be frightened and passive (as a perceived protection);
- have fewer markers and boundaries to help them understand the transition to adulthood;
- have no expectations given to them that they will be involved in choice and decision making;
- be over socialised into conforming, obedient behaviour;
- constantly have expectations made of them which they cannot meet;
- be made fun of because they make mistakes.

As the result of the original cognitive impairment overlaid by the way others behave towards them, people with severe learning disabilities are often:

- passive, as has been described earlier;
- lacking in a sense of self.

We understand who we are through communication with others and through our own mastery of aspects of our world. If young people are unable to master the world they are likely to become:

- lacking in autonomy;
- lacking in instrumentality;
- totally reliant on the directives and judgements of others;
- defensive;
- aggressive;
- unwilling to be instrumental because of fear of failure;
- unable to place any value on their own wishes and options;
- lacking in skills;
- lacking in self-confidence .

In the traditional ways in which adults with severe learning disabilities lived their lives many of these defects did not matter. Many of them were actually an advantage to people who were expected to conform and comply and who were perceived as eternal children and having no entry to the adult world of self-determination, status and rights.

Times, services and expectations are, however changing. The right of people with disabilities to full adult status is increasingly acknowledged. As children with severe learning disabilities are perceived as potential adults, with adult status like that of their peers, their teenage years become more significant. If young people with severe learning disabilities are to be full adults they must work through an adolescent transition.

It is only necessary to consider the goals of adolescence as set out in Chapter 1 to understand the task which confronts all those who wish to support young people with learning disabilities, in making the transition to adulthood.

Physical Maturity

Most young people with severe learning disabilities reach the stages of physical maturity at roughly the same time as their peers, although there is a general feeling that they do not. For example, there are many myths about the sexual maturity of people with Down's Syndrome but a Danish study carried out in the late 80's (Goldstein 1988), comparing a group of young women with Down's Syndrome aged 15 - 20, with a similar group without disabilities, found no significant differences in their ages at the time of their first period, regularity of menstruation, average cycle or average duration of bleeding.

The general feeling that young people with learning disabilities remain children longer, cannot be put down to later physical development. It can however, be ascribed to the fact that the same meaning is not attached to physical developments as it is for other young people.

The development towards sexual maturity can be denied by:

– keeping the same vocabulary, systems and perceptions as were current throughout childhood. This is particularly evident in the speech and actions of some parents and some all-age schools for children with severe learning difficulties.
– styles of dress which either blur all sexual characteristics, for example loose fitting tracksuits or jumpers and jeans etc., which are either very childlike or very middle-aged so that adolescence is denied.

Very few adolescents with severe learning disabilities have clothes which are indistinguishable from those of their non-disabled peers, even though the very marked differences of a few years ago are now rare. It would be very unusual now, for example, to see a young man of sixteen or seventeen dressed in women's synthetic elasticated trousers, or wearing a belted overcoat and a flat cap, even though this was not uncommon in the very recent past.

Most of the clothes worn by the majority of young people with severe learning disabilities are not however, chosen by themselves or other young people of the same age with a view to heightening adolescence. Most adolescents dress to look like adolescents in whatever the prevailing adolescent style happens to be. Most adolescents with severe learning difficulties do not do so. Their adolescence and the physical changes which are part of it, are therefore minimised. Physical maturation is minimised.

Cognitive Maturity

Young people with severe learning difficulties have difficulty understanding the limited world of childhood. They have more difficulty understanding the considerably more complex world of adults and adult expectations.

Society has a set of norms for the competence of adults. They are usually not made explicit but they are deeply embedded and held in common by almost all members of society. They are the things we unthinkingly assume adults can do.
Examples are:

- handle money
- tell the time
- read
- get about independently
- use a telephone
- manage personal care
- make a cup of tea
- tie their own shoe laces
- follow directions or instructions.

People who cannot do these things stand out in the adult world.

Adolescents and adults with severe learning difficulties may find any or all of these things impossible, because of their cognitive impairment and therefore have an inherent difficulty in achieving adult status.

They find it even more difficult if they do not understand that they are emergent adults and do not take on any aspects of adult status.

Questions are often asked, particularly about people with profound and multiple learning disabilities, about whether they can achieve adult status because of the nature and extent of their lack of understanding of the world or ability to function in it.

As has already been noted, most aspects of adult status in our society are earned. They depend on:

– the individual having some skills in these areas;
– other people acknowledging the individual's rights to deploy these skills and to take on responsibility for one's own life.

Traditionally both of these have proved difficult for people with disabilities, particularly where these are very severe. Adults with a disability may have difficulty in achieving adult status because:

– the difficulty itself precludes their achieving the level of general competence generally regarded as necessary for adult status;
– they do not have access to the learning experiences which would enable them to develop greater competence;
– they have potential or actual competence, but their right to use it is not recognised by other people.

Adults with severe intellectual impairment are handicapped in all three areas.

Adults with a profound cognitive impairment which is often accompanied by a physical or sensory disability usually have none of these obvious indicators of adult status.

– they are unable to be responsible for almost any aspect of their lives;
– they need to be washed, dressed, fed, cared for, and guarded against danger by others;
– they are not economically self-sufficient;
– they have no adult roles within the community or the family.

Adult Dignity

Yet they are adults. They have the right to the adult dignity which is an essential element of adulthood. For these learners, dignity and status must be conferred by others, they will not be earned through the usual adult roles and activities. Recognition of a person as an adult learner is an important act in the confirmation of adult dignity, whilst the curriculum itself has a major part to play in establishing status.

A lack of cognitive maturity is not a barrier to adulthood or adult dignity.

Emotional Maturity

Young people with learning difficulties are often prevented from achieving the degree of emotional maturity they are capable of because they are not allowed to experience and build on the very often painful and difficult events which lead to emotional development. They can be protected and kept from being hurt, but then they do not develop. They therefore find it difficult to establish adolescent or adult roles in any relationship.

An Individual Identity

Adolescents with severe learning difficulties are often dependent on others for the meeting of their most basic needs; they find it difficult to separate from care givers and often are unable to challenge their views and decisions. A separate individual identity is difficult to achieve in these circumstances.

Emancipation from parents and from childhood

Many young people or indeed adults, with severe learning disabilities are genuinely dependent on their parents in many aspects of their lives. They do not have the competence and capacity for independence and autonomy of their peers. Yet they need to develop some degree of emotional independence and an individual adult identity if they are to make the transition to elements of adult status.

The curriculum in schools, colleges, training and work programmes must address these care issues for transition. If they do not do so successfully, all the work they do, however successful, may be valueless. For a young person to make a choice, he needs not only the concept of choice and the skills to make one, he needs to see himself, and be seen by others as a choice-maker. That is what this book addresses.

Those who live and work with them must also make a transition in terms of their own thinking and in their perception and treatment of the young people. This is no different from the adjustments which must be made in attitudes towards all young people as they become adults, but it is a relatively new concept for those involved with young people with significant learning disabilities.

Chapter 4 examines the role of school in enabling young people to enter the adolescent transition.

Chapter 5 looks at the development which further education can achieve and the ways in which it can support and extend adolescent development.

Chapter 7 focuses on the end states of the transition as young people move into the world of work or day services.

Each stage of the transition is vital, if it is to proceed successfully and young people with severe learning disabilities are to achieve their rightful status and dignity as adults.

CHAPTER 3

CURRENT SERVICES FOR ADOLESCENTS

Most services received by young people with severe learning difficulties are defined in law.

Education is the major service provided for young people under the age of 19. Until that age every individual is entitled to a free full-time place in education.

Education has the major role in preparing young people for the adolescent transition and for adult life.

Young people are moving from school to adult life in a society which has changed radically in the last ten years and is still changing. New laws have been important but even more important perhaps, has been new political attitudes and social policies. This chapter will focus on some of the more recent legislation and its possible effects on the services and transition of young people with learning difficulties.

Since 1979 the government has introduced major legislative changes in education, health and social services and in the social security system. Employment training for a changing labour market has also been the subject of changes in the law. Under-pinning all the initiatives that have been taken is a concept of reduced responsibilities for local authorities and increased responsibilities for individuals. This will of course, have an impact on the services which can be provided to support young people with severe learning difficulties as they make the transition to adult life.

The government has increased its powers of overall control. At the same time it has delegated many responsibilities elsewhere. Responsibilities have been delegated to governors for example, in schools and to the corporations which now govern further education colleges in the new educational system.

Young people and adults receive a range of services which aim to support them but there is very little evidence in this country of a coherent policy of support or evidence of much co-operation of practice across departments either at a national or at a local level. The need for interagency collaboration is taken up again in Chapter 9 of this book.

EDUCATIONAL LEGISLATION

The Education Act (1981)

The 1981 Education Act was implemented in 1983. This Act moved away from categories of handicap to a concept of 'special educational need'. Special educational needs were defined as learning difficulties.

These learning difficulties of all kinds had to be significantly greater than those of the majority of children of the same age or the result of disabilities which prevented a child from using the facilities generally available to the majority of children in their area. The Act made it clear that primary and secondary schools were responsible for meeting educational needs, particularly the broad range of learning difficulties commonly found in the school population.

For children with more severe and complex learning difficulties new procedures of assessment and for making a Statement of special educational needs were set out in detail in this Act. Statements, which should be agreed by parents and reviewed annually, cover the school period up to the age of 19. However if a young person leaves school before the age of 19 and enters further education, the provision of the Statement does not apply.

The Statement of special educational needs entitles a child to receive the support he or she needs to succeed in education. The Statement should be reviewed annually to ensure that the support a child is actually entitled to matches his needs at a particular period of time.

It is particularly important that during the adolescent years the Statement should reflect a young person's need for support at this particular time. For young people who are at school the Statement of special educational needs can be an important support in their transition towards adult life.

The Education Act 1981 has been substantially rewritten but the concept of the Statement of special educational needs providing a valuable support service to young people during their adolescent years if they remain at school, is still fundamental to educational legislation.

The Education Reform Act (1988)

This act dealt with all aspects of education managed by local education authorities including schools, further and higher, and adult education. Its aim was to raise standards in education. A major means for doing this was the introduction of a national curriculum, and national assessments at the ages of 7, 11, 14 and 16.

The Act also introduced a delegation of resources and responsibilities to the governing bodies of schools and the reduction of the direct involvement of local education authorities in administration and provision.

The National Curriculum ensures the same core of subjects is offered to all pupils between the ages of 5 and 16.

Although the introduction of the National Curriculum has broadened the range of subjects on offer to children and young people with severe learning difficulties, its impact also means that there is less time available for life and social skills and for much of the work which young people need to support their adolescent transition.

The Further and Higher Education Act (1992)

This Act changed substantially the way in which further education, for young people over the age of 16 who have left school, is run in this country. Local education authorities no longer have a role in running colleges of further education or sixth form colleges. They are now run by corporations which were developed from existing governing bodies. Each corporation has responsibility for the college it runs. The quality of college provision is monitored by the Further Education Funding Council through its inspectorate. Each college is required to have a strategic plan. The strategic plan must include the college's plans to provide for students with learning difficulties and or disabilities.

 The role of education in preparing young people for adolescence and adulthood is crucial. Education is not however, the sole provider of services for adolescents and young adults with learning difficulties. Legislation in other areas has an important role to play, particularly in the assessment of the needs of young people as they move through their adolescent years.

Disabled persons (Services Consultation and Representation) Act (1986)

This Act has only been implemented in part. Sections 5 and 6 are about the preparation of a plan for leaving school, interagency co-operation in the production of this plan and putting it into effect. These sections were implemented in 1988. The intention of sections 5 and 6 of the Disabled Persons Act was to act as a bridge between education and provision made by departments of social services.

The definition of disability used, however, in the Act dates from 1948 and the terminology used is no longer acceptable to many people. One result of the narrow definitions used is that only a small proportion of those who have had their special educational needs met in school can expect to receive provision from social services. This Act does recognise some aspects of planning for transition and the need for the advocacy of individual needs.

The Children Act (1989)

This Act, which was implemented in late 1991, replaced a mass of existing fragmented legislation with a clear overall framework. It simplified court procedures, increased and clarified the concept of parental responsibility and introduced a category of children in need among whom children with disabilities are included. The 1948 definitions are again used to define disability. Children with disabilities are clearly stated to be children first, and one of the aims of parts of the act is to ensure that they are entitled to as normal a life as possible. Planning for transition is included under the scope of The Children Act.

The NHS and Community Care Act (1990)

The NHS and Community Care Act sets out proposals for community care. The resourcing and management of care and the new responsibilities of local authorities to manage rather than provide will take a long time to be fully effective. However, the general thrust of the Act is very much in keeping with the concept of adult status and of the transitions in adolescence which are therefore needed to enable people to become fully adult.

THE LAW IN PRACTICE: the services adolescents actually receive

Almost all young people with severe learning difficulties attend special schools. These may be designated as special schools for children with severe learning difficulties or they may be more general in their intake. In many parts of the country schools for children with severe learning difficulties are all-age with children starting school at 2 or 3 years of age and remaining in the same school until they leave at the age of 19. There are however, an increasing number of variations. In some parts of the country schools are now split so that they have separate primary and secondary departments. There are also education authorities where all young people leave school at 16 and where provision is made in further education for all adolescents between the ages of 16 and 19.

Further education colleges offer a range of provision. Each college which offers this provision has opted along its own lines to suit the facilities which it has to offer and the particular demands made on it by schools and by parents.

Most college courses include teaching aimed at developing the following:

1. An awareness of self
2. An awareness of others
3. Appropriate adolescent or young adult behaviours and relationships
4. Choice and decision making
5. New skills especially leisure skills
6. The beginning of self advocacy
7. An awareness of the community and its facilities
8. Risk-taking
9. Self care
10. The concept of the student's changing role within the family.

A few colleges operate a system whereby they are willing to take on a student with any degree of learning disability and have the facilities of the staffing to cope with the needs of these young people. Others however operate a selection process based on levels of maturity which are considered to be necessary to cope with a particular college.

CHAPTER 4

THE SCHOOL CURRICULUM

Schools provide the starting point for transition.

Schools are usually seen as synonymous with childhood, but young people move through at least one and possibly two phases of adolescent development while they are at school.

By the end of their school days young people will almost certainly have moved through the early adolescent phase.

They will have :

- entered or moved through the physical changes of puberty;
- lost most childhood exemption from being responsible for their own actions;
- a clear view of themselves as no longer children and as being emergent adults.

Young people with severe learning difficulties will usually have fewer markers of these transitions than other young people and will actually need larger, clearer markers than others. The School Curriculum needs to point out and make sense of all indications of adolescence in an adolescent appropriate way.

Physical changes

Physical changes should be pointed out to young people and explained as they occur. This should, of course be done sensitively and appropriately either individually or in same sex groups.

Young women should be told that they are developing breasts, starting to have periods and growing body hair because they are becoming women and physically capable of having babies. They may need clear explanations, however, that they will not have babies spontaneously, but only as a result of sexual intercourse.

Young men should know that their own bodily changes are again because they are growing up and that the growth of their penis and testicles are because they will produce the sperm that can begin the development of a baby if they have sexual intercourse.

These individual pointers should be in addition to the formal group sex education sessions which most schools provide as part of the curriculum. Group sessions are important for gaining information but individuals need to have the changes their own bodies are going through pointed out to them and made sense of in terms of adolescence.

School staff should work in close partnership with parents in these very personal aspects of sex education. Parents should, of course, be kept fully informed as to the school approach.

All such personal conversations should be :

- planned and recorded;
- carried out in a matter of fact way;
- encouraging and supportive;
- clearly part of an educational process;
- carried out by an appropriate person in an appropriate setting.

Other changes

Other changes need to be highlighted equally clearly.
For example:

- the need to wear appropriate clothes;
- the need to behave differently;
- the perceptions of others.

Inappropriate behaviour, for example over-familiarity, excessive physical closeness or childlike behaviour should be discouraged and a clear, simple explanation given that the individual is now too grown up to behave in that way and that they are embarrassing other people.

Self Advocacy

All young people need to learn how to make their choices known to others and at a later stage of their development how to argue their case in discussion. The delivery of the curriculum should include genuine opportunities to express preferences, to make decisions and to make a reasoned case for decisions.

If young people are to have a quality of life as adults they should be able to hold their own preferences even when these are disapproved of by others. However, an aspect of choice making in schools which often needs development is that where the choice which a young person makes is one that's felt not to be in his or her best interest by parents and teachers. This concept is something that schools may wish to explore and include in their policy on issues for transition.

Working together

Traditionally children and young people in schools for those with severe learning difficulties have worked on individual tasks. The structure of the National Curriculum has to some extent had an impact on this process but many young people find it difficult to enter an adolescent sub-group because of their lack of experience of spending time in groups with their peers. Schools should offer all young people the opportunity for working and being together in groups without adult intervention.

Employment

It is becoming increasingly clear that many young people with severe learning difficulties are able to maintain themselves in open employment in the community if they receive appropriate education, training and support. Employment should not be ruled out as a legitimate objective for young people with severe learning difficulties. Programmes at school should include vocational preparation, training in real work situations, regular interaction with non-disabled contemporaries and experiences which enable appropriate employment to be chosen.

Independent living

Skills necessary to live independently in the community should be developed as part of the school curriculum. They should be taught and practised in natural situations including residential settings. The teaching programme should involve a variety of different people and places in the community.

Interaction with people without disabilities

Even when young people with disabilities attend the same school with others who do not have disabilities, interaction cannot be assumed to be taking place. Regular interaction between young people with and without disabilities needs to be planned and should be an integral part of a transitional curriculum. Without such opportunities young people may not be able to participate successfully in the community and thus be barred from adult status.

Teaching priorities

Where the teacher has a choice of the skills and knowledge to be taught, it is important to consider the objectives of transition. Particularly when working with those who have severe learning difficulties priority should be given to the development of skills relevant to independent functioning within an integrated community setting. This may mean that for the duration of the transitional programme there is a lack of time for other activities such as art, music, drama and other creative aspects of the curriculum. These can however, be successfully reincorporated into learning once young people have made the all-important transition to adult status.

Effective teaching for transition should encourage student choice and individual preferences. The curriculum should include a commitment to personal support during transition, experience of integration in the local environment, real work in integrated settings and the effective use of community resources.

For young people under the age of sixteen teachers face the difficult task of developing these aspects of transition while maintaining the principles of the framework of the National Curriculum. At this stage the demands of the National Curriculum will take priority as is appropriate in this early stage of transition. When a young person reaches the age of sixteen and moves outside the framework of the National Curriculum, the skills and competencies necessary for living and working as independently as possible in the community will expand and take over a much larger part of the curriculum for transition.

CHAPTER 5

FURTHER EDUCATION

All provision for young people in further education is centred on transition.

For any young person a course at college or university provides both a particular set of skills and a period of transition.   This period of transition enables them to move from the dependent role in the school-based world of childhood to an autonomous and independent role in the adult world.

This transition takes place on two levels:

1. Through changing perceptions of self within the student as he or she develops and matures in a new and more demanding environment.

2. As a result of the changing perceptions of society of the young person as he or she moves into a more independent role which is seen as bringing him or her onto equal terms with full adults.

In the past most young people with severe learning difficulties have not made this transition either through a college course or by starting work and so as mature adults they retain all the components of a childhood role; dependence, passivity, submissiveness naivety and childlike behaviour. As adults they still think of themselves as children and society as a whole reinforces and is reinforced in this belief.

The major role of further education is to stimulate or extend such young people into their adolescent transition and enable them to make best use of this period of transition so that it will end with as many as possible of this group having a clearly defined image of themselves as fully adult. Society should also have a similar concept of this group of people, as being adults with difficulties rather than as post-pubescent children.

Further and continuing education opportunities for those with the full range of learning difficulties have increased over the past ten to fifteen years. They still vary from area to area but an increasing number of colleges now make further education available to a wider range of learners, sometimes in conjunction with social and health services or voluntary organisations.

A pattern of provision can be identified which is either full or part time.

Full time courses are:

- usually for school leavers aged between sixteen and twenty one years;
- usually up to three years in length;
- based at a college of further education or tertiary college;
- varied in content according to whatever facilities the individual college has on offer;
- based on two major concepts:
  - personal development
  - transition to adult life
- very occasionally designed for adults.

Full time adult courses are based on personal development and transitions within adult life and often for people who had no opportunity to make a real adolescent transition at the appropriate age.

Most full time courses for students with severe learning difficulties aim to give them some of the skills, opportunities and beliefs about themselves that will promote adult status.

Core skills include:

1. *Self care:* cooking, shopping and care of the environment in ways that are appropriate to adolescents and young adults. Travelling and being able to self correct and learn from mistakes. These skills enable individuals to take on more responsibility for their own lives.

2. *Skills for employability:* which can open the doors to productive activity and lead to people being able to earn their own money in an adult environment.

3. *Opportunities to develop adolescent and adult relationships:* to operate in an adult setting and to engage in a range of leisure activities which enable people to both become and be seen as adults.

4. *Opportunities to develop adult self concepts:* including specific teaching about adult status and work with families and carers on adult status which enables the students to think of themselves as adults and also to be treated as adults by the most important people in their lives.

These cores of activities focus on the areas of adult status which are identified in Chapter 1. Part time provision may be delivered through outreach services to where people live or where they have other daytime activities. They may be based in a college or in an adult institute or centre; they may be in special classes or through supported access to mainstream classes. They may be available to young people who are still at school, those who have recently left school and to adults throughout their lives.

Further education should aim to meet needs by offering an individually tailored educational programme, which is properly constructed within a curriculum framework, which uses age appropriate activities, language, materials and teaching strategies. Technological support may have a vital part to play. Such a programme will stretch and challenge each learner within a supportive setting. This definition of further education should apply to every student within the college, not only to those who have learning difficulties. Care must be taken however to ensure that all students particularly those with severe learning difficulties are included within this framework.

Further education provision for students with severe learning difficulties should expect to be judged by the quality of the transition that it enables young people to make. This can best be achieved by assessing their needs very thoroughly, devising a strategy to ensure that as many as possible of those needs are met in the time available by accurate record keeping and by reassessing needs as students develop.

CHAPTER 6

EDUCATION AND TRAINING FOR WORK

The entry to the world of work can mark the end of the transitional process.

Young people with disabilities encounter the same difficulties in transition to adulthood as their peers without disabilities. There can be no doubt that they also face additional difficulties. Disability has, potentially, a profound effect on transition into a working adult life.

In 1977 a survey conducted by the National Children's Bureau identified an unemployment rate of 19.1 per cent amongst disabled school-leavers, compared with 4.4 per cent amongst school-leavers generally. With the rise in the unemployment rate, such a survey today would produce a higher figure. There is a need for another exercise to update information on school-leavers with disabilities.

The official unemployment rate is also affected by the fact that, to be included, an individual has to be both without a job *and* seeking work. Many severely disabled young people are not, therefore, included because they are considered to be outside the employment market by virtue of their disability. Since they are not seen as job-seekers, they are not included in the unemployment statistics, even though they are without paid employment.

Additional Difficulties

The NACEDP Working Party (1986) identified seven areas of difficulty which young people with disabilities have to face over and above the difficulties faced in transition by their peers. These were:

i) At the end of compulsory schooling, some young people are less well equipped than their able-bodied peers with the basic vocational and technical skills needed to enter the labour market.

ii) Young people with disabilities tend to be less mature and their social skills less developed than many of their non-disabled peers.

iii) Before they can settle in employment, many young people with disabilities need organised support from social and medical services.

iv) Some young people have to overcome physical barriers to employment. This may include transport to and from work, as well as access to and within the work place.

v) Some young disabled people have to overcome internal and external psychological barriers to employment.

vi) There is a clear lack of understanding about disabled people amongst many of those providing vocational education and training and amongst employers and their employees.

These are the issues further education and other work preparation agencies must address.

Additional Needs for Support

Because of these extra difficulties, young people with disabilities need additional support in preparing for employment.

Items (i) and (ii) above need to be considered carefully by:

– schools;
– colleges of further education;
– Youth Training Schemes;
– specialist agencies which have a role in preparing young people with disabilities for employment, both before and during their transition into adult life.

The implications of the NACEDP report for vocational education and training

The findings of NACEDP have considerable implications for the curriculum offered by both programmes for school leavers and provision in further education which are designed for, or include, young people with disabilities.

The curriculum, both in its content and its process, should equip young people with disabilities with social, vocational and technical skills. These would enable them to compete on more equal terms with their peers. This is particularly important for young people who do not have cognitive difficulties, when abilities may be unrealised if access is only to a restricted curriculum.

In Handicapped Youth at Work (OECD/CERI 1985), it appears that the needs of the young people interviewed were no better met either by segregated or integrated education. Both kinds of educational provision, therefore, need to examine their present offer.

Special schools need to extend their curricula and avoid over-protection. Other 'mainstream' schools need to provide more effective support which will enable young people with disabilities to gain more from the curriculum on offer.

The Curriculum for Transition

The pre-vocational education and training of young people with disabilities will take place, whether in school, college or Youth Training Scheme, in one of the following ways:

– *Through the specially designed curriculum.*
   This is most appropriate for young people with a cognitive impairment or those with complex disabilities.
– *Through access to the mainstream curriculum.*
   Special schools, college courses or YT, which provide access to all or parts of the mainstream curriculum on their own site or within consortium arrangements, enable young people to have access to the same curriculum offer as their peers. E.g. A programme for students with learning difficulties, which takes place in the mainstream college.
– *Within mainstream provision.*
   Young people are prepared for work in a range of supported mainstream settings.

The Empowering Curriculum

However a young person is prepared for employment, and whatever the content of the programme, the curriculum must:

– empower the students;
– give them the skills to make choices and decisions;
– provide them with the social skills which will be of genuine benefit to them in an unsegregated adult setting such as employment;
– provide the sort of experiences that will trigger and support adolescent transition. Other young people will gain these experiences

outside the curriculum but a young person with disabilities may need the support of school or college. These experiences will include:

- the opportunity for decision making
- appropriate risk taking
- self-advocacy
- freedom for adolescent behaviour
- other appropriate activities.

Rather than handicapping the young person, the curriculum will then serve to empower her or him.

What Must be Avoided?

Where a specifically designed curriculum is delivered, it can sometimes become divorced from the realities of the outside world because of the degree of specialisation necessary.

Special schools and specially designed courses in further education need to review their offer to ensure that it is in line with mainstream provision.

Segregated provision can produce a watered-down or divergent alternative delivered by teachers who often have no contact with their mainstream colleagues and no access to the pre-service and in-service training provided for those involved in the delivery of pre-vocational education.

Support can be managed so ineffectively that it can handicap the young people in their development of autonomy and instrumentality. A classroom assistant, for example, provided to help young blind people manage their environment may effectively divorce them from that peer group and maintain their dependence on an adult long after this has ceased to be appropriate.

The assumption must be challenged that young people with disabilities have had the same life experiences as their non-disabled peers. They may have had little or no opportunity for autonomy outside school or college and been doubly disadvantaged both by the nature of their impairment and by the handicapping effects of society's expectations.

The Benefits of the Empowering Curriculum

If an empowering curriculum were delivered by schools, colleges and Youth Training Schemes, young people with disabilities would be less disadvantaged in their transition to employment. They would be better equipped with the basic vocational and technical skills needed to enter the labour market, more mature, and have better social skills. Furthermore, they would be better fitted to compete with their non-disabled peers.

A NACEDP conclusion - that some young disabled people have to overcome internal psychological barriers to employment - should also be addressed through the empowering curriculum.

It is emphasised in *Obstacles to Work for All* (OECD/CERI, 1983) that, unless the barriers to early expectations of full adult status are challenged, young people with disabilities may be cocooned by their families and by caring services. They may be reluctant to venture into the unfamiliar environment of work and adult status. This would, of course, severely handicap young people in developing a positive determination to seek and sustain employment. It may be easier and feel safer to remain dependent.

The empowering curriculum should not be seen as relevant only to education. It is vital that programmes delivered by T.E.E.D. also recognise these issues. Schemes should acknowledge that young people with disabilities may need particular support in developing an adult worker identity.

Current Employment in the UK

If you are preparing young people with learning difficulties for employment, you need to be very aware of what actual opportunities there are for work.

Unemployment statistics are used to denote only those people who do not have paid work but are actively seeking it. This means that the number of people with disabilities who *would* wish to work if support were available remains hidden.

All young people seeking employment enter a particular job market. The state of that market and the factors which have operated in bringing about current trends have a fundamental effect on the range of options open to them.

Young people seeking employment in the UK today are faced with a very different employment world from that which awaited their parents at a similar age.

Unemployment reached a peak in the mid 1980's when, in the summer of 1986, the figure reached 3.133 million (Department of Employment figures) - over 11 per cent of those people who were defined as being within the employment market. Since that time the seasonally adjusted rate has fallen 32 times in succession and the cumulative fall to date has been 1.215 million (*Guardian*, 1989). This puts the *official* total of unemployed people at present at 1.918 million (Department of Employment, 13th March 1989), an unemployment rate of 6.9 per cent - as compared with 4.8 per cent in 1979.

However, a relatively small number of people are unemployed long-term as compared to the total number. Most individuals' experience of unemployment is of the lengthening gaps between work rather than of continuous spells of being unemployed (Daniel, 1981).

The current rate of unemployment is such, however, that there is a very real chance that a young person may not have a job or may be under pressure to stay in one job rather than explore a number of different ones.

This limits the exploration of different vocational paths in a way that makes the early years of employment for a young person a very different experience from that of the 1960's. At that time Super et al (1967) found that a significant number of young people spent some time changing career direction and moving from job to job between the ages of 18 and 25. This is supported by Gibbons and Lohnes (1969): between a third and a half of the young people they studied were still moving from job to job and had not stabilized their working life by the age of 25.

This exploration of different jobs before making a commitment would be much more risky today. What is more, a record of changing jobs could result in a young person being considered unreliable and unemployable. A young person's initial choice of job thus has far more significance.

Preparation and training must support young people by attempting to help them *sample* a range of vocational areas before actually committing themselves to real employment. Most early vocational education and training in the UK at present (Cooper, 1989 for an overview) aims to fulfil this need.

In the UK, unemployment is now less acute nationally than it was two or three years ago, but this mean figure conceals many pockets of high unemployment, both in certain geographical areas and amongst certain groups within the population. For example, a laundry which provided 50 jobs may close and instead two estate agents, three specialist retail outlets for electronic goods, a restaurant and a solicitor's office may open in the same area. There will have been no statistical job loss, but most of the ex-laundry employees may become unemployed because they cannot be recruited for the new jobs. New arrivals or commuters from another area fill them. This has implications both for geographical areas and for certain groups of job seekers.

The current unemployment situation and the changes which have taken place over the past two or three decades are examined below in order to illustrate current trends in the world of work which will be encountered by young people entering, or already in, employment.

It is difficult to obtain a clear picture of the employment situation. There is considerable disagreement as to whether there has been such a fall in the number of registered unemployed people as the official figures indicate. Some commentators argue that the fall has been brought about, not by a growth in the number of jobs available, but by other factors. These include changing the ways in which the statistics are formulated, and the growth of training schemes such as the Youth Training Scheme and Employment Training. If people are taking part in these schemes, they are not registered as unemployed, but neither do they have permanent jobs. It is not intended to explore this further here, but the arguments are worth noting.

Whatever the increase in the actual number of jobs may have been in recent years, there can be no doubt that jobs themselves have changed and are changing.

Unemployment is not caused by simple shrinkage in the number of jobs available so that those seeking work outnumber the available posts. Massey and Meegan's (1982) analysis of the reasons for job losses in the two decades leading up to the early 1980's is helpful in clarifying this. They argue that jobs which have been created since then differ, both in quantity and quality from employment opportunities previously available. They describe the process, which has resulted in a major shift in the number and in the kind of jobs which are available currently.

They identify three main elements:

- rationalisation;
- intensification;
- investment and technical change;

which are not of course, mutually exclusive.

RATIONALISATION

What does it mean?

Job loss is linked to loss of output. Many manufacturing and construction industries do not, for example, need as large a work-force as 30 years ago. The decline began in the mid-1960's and by the mid-1970's, manufacturing in the UK employed 1.3 million fewer people than ten years earlier, a decline of just over 15 per cent (Brown and Sheriff, 1978).

Effect on the work-force

- Considerably fewer jobs are available in particular industries.
- There are very high levels of unemployment in the areas where these and similar industries have been major employers.

Certain parts of the country and indeed particular towns and cities, have been severely affected by rationalisation, and young people coming into the job market in these areas, such as South Tyneside or Northern Ireland, are particularly disadvantaged as few alternatives to traditional sources of employment have been developed.

INTENSIFICATION

What does it mean?

Fewer workers maintain the previous level of output without major changes to either the nature of the work or the scale of production.

Each worker has to achieve more output in a given amount of time. This can be achieved by:

- additional work aids
- speeding up the process
- changes in working practices
- increased flexibility of the workforce
- the payment of bonuses.

Effect on the workforce

Fast, efficient workers are needed who can maintain output, possibly across a range of activities. Fewer jobs are available for slower, less flexible workers who are efficient only in one activity or part of the process.

INVESTMENT AND TECHNICAL CHANGE

What does it mean?

Job losses occur as the result of significant investment, often related to changes in techniques of production. In 16 of the 31 industries studied by Massey and Meegan, job losses followed heavy capital investment. Unlike intensification where the worker is able to reduce the time devoted to the production activity, the activity itself is taken over by machinery or equipment.

Some industries' technical change was brought about either by the introduction of machinery, or by replacement of existing machinery with more sophisticated and extensive equipment. Some industries were influenced considerably by the introduction of new technology which reached the UK and other industrialised countries at a time of severe recession. (Benson and Lloyd, 1983).

Information technology was seen as a major threat to jobs and at the end of the 1970's it was believed that five million people in the UK might become unemployed during the 1980's as a direct result of the adoption of the new technology. (Hines and Searle, 1979).

Effect on the workforce

There was an overestimate of the speed of change in technologically conservative Britain, but it is certain that the impact of micro-technology will continue to be very considerable. The training and retraining of workers is a necessity. For this to be successful, higher levels of basic education, flexibility and transferable skills are needed than for many of the semi- or unskilled jobs which have not been replaced. Traditional jobs disappear, new and different ones are created.

OUTCOMES OF THESE CHANGES

These three elements operating within the employment market have together produced and are still producing, changes in the requirements which many employers have of their work-force. There are young people who would have been able to find appropriate jobs 20 or 30 years ago, but who lack the speed, flexibility, transferable skills or general education for the jobs which are on offer as a result of intensification or technical change.

SERVICE INDUSTRIES

Service industries have not followed an identical path. During the 1960's and 1970's the decline in the work-force in service industries was slower, and in some areas, such as London and the South East, loss of jobs in manufacturing has been more than compensated for by gains in service sector jobs.

Growth in this sector has also provided a counterbalance to manufacturing and construction industry decline, although in some areas there has been total, or almost total loss of manufacturing jobs with no growth in service sector employment, (Layard, 1986). However, nationally, service industries are likely to provide a significantly higher number of new opportunities than manufacturing industries.

The situation in the UK is not markedly dissimilar to other European countries, although the UK unemployment rate has been higher in the 1980's (OECD, 1985). In the USA however, the pattern is and has been, different. During the 1970's there was a rapid expansion in the number of jobs. This growth rate slowed in the early 1980's. From 1983 onward, unemployment was reduced until in 1986 it was at the same level as in 1979 (Layard, 1986). The trend away from manufacturing to an increased number of jobs in the service sector has been similar.

Rothschild (1981) notes that many service sector jobs offer lower rates of pay per hour, fewer hours of work and less possibility of advancement than had been previously available.

WHO IS MOST AFFECTED BY THESE TRENDS?

Three groups of people are likely to be hardest hit by these changes:

– young people;
– unskilled workers;
– people with disabilities, especially learning disabilities.

Young people will need considerable experience in the workplace before they are able to work efficiently at speed and develop a range of flexible skills. Training can be carried out during the Youth Training Scheme but most young people will still be at a disadvantage compared with experienced workers.

Many employers also feel that older workers will be more reliable and stable. This disadvantage is shown clearly in the statistics of unemployment, where the rate is much higher for young people than for older people. In 1985 (OPCS, 1985) male unemployment rates were 22.3 per cent, 29.2 per cent and 22.5 per cent in the age groups under 18, 18 - 19 and 20 - 24 respectively, while those for men aged 25 - 54 and 55 - 59 years were 13.7 per cent and 18.7 per cent.

Semi- and unskilled workers and young people who would seek this kind of work can be disadvantaged by the changes. In Britain in 1983, 84 per cent of unemployed men were manual workers, half of them semi- or unskilled. Amongst these groups, unemployment rates were (OPCS, 1983):

- Non-manual   5 per cent
- Semi-manual   2 per cent
- Semi- and unskilled   23 per cent

Ten or fifteen years previously semi- and unskilled workers were about four times as likely to be unemployed as non-manual workers. (Micklewright, 1983).

People with disabilities tend to be:

- less well educated;
- less well trained;
- slower because of their disability. (OECD/CERI, 1985)

The OECD/CERI work referred to above, points out that the low standards and expectations of special schools and the lack of effective teaching in mainstream schools are equally unsatisfactory. They both represent a failure to assist young people in their development and serve instead, to limit their life chances.

They are less likely to be able to meet the demands of employers resulting from intensification and technological change. They are likely to be further disadvantaged by prejudice from employers.

CONCLUSIONS

Those young people who are not only disadvantaged by their lack of experience and personal maturity, but who also have a disability are likely to face considerable difficulty in obtaining employment without individual support.

Those people who are young, with learning difficulties and likely to be seeking unskilled work, will need intensive preparation and support if they are to gain and keep employment.

These conclusions are supported by Marshall (1978) who says that the young people who are most likely to experience difficulty in securing a first job, who are most likely to be unemployed more often and for longer periods, and those who have the most socio-economic disadvantages are: the poorly educated; the physically disabled; the mentally handicapped and young mothers.

Trends in the job market mean that potential employees are particularly in need of support from education and training to equip them to take on the available jobs, which may demand flexibility, transferable or technical skills, or may require the personal qualities and interpersonal skills needed for the service industries. Retraining will be necessary to equip people for periodic career change.

Youth employment is a major aspect of the overall picture. It particularly affects young people who are educationally, socially and economically disadvantaged and unless effective measures are taken to tackle their unemployment problems, they will become *permanently* dependent on benefits, and *permanently* deprived of a major marker of adult status and of active and equal participation in the mainstream of an industrialised society.

It is vital that all young people have access to an educational and training curriculum that will genuinely equip them for adult life. It is particularly important that young people who are at a disadvantage have access to available support.

WHY IS WORK VALUED SO HIGHLY ?

Employment is valued for itself and for what it can provide. The work can give satisfaction but many workers do not seem to feel that their job is satisfying in itself.

When Blauner (1960) asked workers whether they would choose the same occupation again, he found that although 80 per cent of mathematicians, lawyers and journalists said they would make the same choice, less that 22 per cent of unskilled car and steel workers gave the same reply. Although they did not wish to stop working, they did not feel that the work they were engaged in was enjoyable in itself.

Even when job satisfaction is low, however, work fulfils many of the requirements of adult status. It provides an income which enables the individual to be economically self-sufficient and therefore able to:

- set up an independent household;
- make choices of clothing and activities which parents would refuse to finance;
- have an active social life;
- take responsibility for providing for others.

Other areas in which work contributes to adult status are described in *Disabled Youth : A Right to Adult Status* (OECD/CERI, 1988) as:

- personal identity,
- self-esteem,
- responsibility,
- dignity,
- acceptance as an adult in society;

as well as other major functions such as:

- the feeling that a person is making a contribution to the community;
- providing opportunities for meeting new people;
- providing a structure and regular routine for the day;
- providing a context in which a young person can learn to be an adult and take on adult roles.

In Project Paper 50 *An Ordinary Working Life* (Kings Fund. 1984), the authors also associate work with a variety of gains:

- status as a worker and an adult;
- a structure to one's life;
- control over one's life;
- daytime occupation;
- social relationships;
- a valued self-image;

as well as with an income.

These views are shared by other writers, including Wansbrough and Cooper, (1980), who look at the additional gains which young people with disabilities receive from employment.

Work provides:

- A way of shedding one's disabled status and joining the normal world of workers.
- A visible measure of normality. There are few other such visible ways in which young disabled people can demonstrate their abilities.
- Self-esteem, which comes from making a contribution rather than being a recipient.
- Identification as a worker proves one's ability to meet society's expectations of an adult. These are particularly important for young people who may be more dependent in some areas of life than their peers, in a culture which places a low value on dependency and a high value on autonomy.

There are major implications for young people with disabilities who want to work and who are unable to obtain or sustain paid employment. In common with their non-disabled peers, they are likely to experience:

- lack of money or poverty;
- low status in society;
- low self-esteem;
- decreased structure in their lives;
- decreased control over their lives;
- fewer choices of daytime occupation;
- few opportunities for responsibility;
- perceived lack of dignity;
- impoverished social contact;
- lack of a valued self-image;
- lack of acceptance as an adult in society.

In short, this is an impoverishment of many of the factors which give meaning to adult life and which are gained either through employment or through other legitimate roles such as being a student or mother.

For young people with disabilities however, there will be additional difficulties in challenging the child-like, financially and socially dependent role traditionally allocated to many people with disabilities. If they are deprived of access to employment as a major marker of adult status and in addition, are unable to demonstrate their abilities in other fully adult roles, there is apparently no alternative but to take on the role of 'disabled person' with all its connotations.

People with disabilities, particularly where these are relatively severe, have been accorded less than full adult status and are generally regarded as incapable of taking on the adult role of employee:

> ...as long as I was in the protective custody of family life or college schedules and lived without exercising my rights as an adult citizen, the forces of society were kind and unruffling. It was after college, business schools and innumerable stretches as a volunteer worker on community projects, that I was often bogged down by the medieval prejudices and superstitions of the business world. Looking for a job was like standing before a firing squad. Employers were shocked that I had the gall to apply for a job. (Young person with disabilities quoted in Henrick and Kreigel, 1961).

Perhaps the shock felt by the employers was a response to a person with a disability trying to become a full adult and not amazement that such a person had the skills necessary for the job.

CONCLUSION

There are many aspects of adult status in our society. A range of these can be achieved through paid employment. Lack of employment can make it difficult to gain access to full adult status, particularly when unemployment is not positively chosen as an alternative lifestyle.

Young people who are both disabled and unemployed face enormous barriers in the transition to active adult life. Unless we, as a society, are willing to accept the challenge of providing each individual with the support needed to gain and sustain employment we are guilty of denying access to what is generally regarded as full adult status.

Strategies and resources must be found by which young people with disabilities can not only become contributing members of society through employment, if that is at all possible, but also achieve a range of fully adult roles in society, whether or not they are in employment.

PERCEPTIONS OF EMPLOYABILITY

In the study for *Enabled to Work*, (FEU 1989), employers were interviewed about their experiences of employing workers with a disability. Representatives of preparation and placement agencies were also interviewed in order to compare their concepts of employment competence with those of the employers themselves. During the course of the interviews it became clear that a general notion of employability exists, and that there was a consensus about the general requirements which a young person needs to meet in order to be employable. This generally agreed 'Employability Package' is set out below.

In order to be employable it is thought that a young person should be:

- reliable;
- conscientious;
- motivated to work;
- able to relate to colleagues;
- able to get to and from work;
- able to understand and carry out instructions;
- acceptable in terms of personal hygiene and self-presentation;
- acceptable in terms of social behaviour;
- able to respond pleasantly and co-operatively;
- able to survive in the world of work;
- able to work without constant supervision;
- able to take the initiative;
- able to keep work separate from other aspects of their life;
- possessed of an appropriate degree of personal autonomy.

Reliability

Everyone interviewed considered reliability, in the sense of timekeeping, regular attendance and dependability, to be vital in employment.

It was also seen as an important factor in preparation for employment and agencies which did not require it were viewed as providing poor training. Two employers gave their perspective:

> We have had young people we couldn't keep because of their inability to understand basic job requirements of regular attendance and timekeeping.

> We once had a school-based work-experience scheme which left it to individuals to turn up or not and provided them with no learning structure.

Conscientiousness

This was rated as more important than speed by most employers. For example:

> I look for steadiness rather than speed. Keeping going is more important than speed of work.

There is undoubtedly, however, a degree of slowness in performing tasks which is unacceptable.

Employees were required who:

- had a conscientious attitude;
- understood the personal responsibilities involved in contractual employment;
- had the ability to concentrate for long enough to produce useful work.

Responsibility towards a job

There was general agreement that some young people failed to sustain employment because they did not have a real commitment to the work and to their colleagues. This apparent lack of responsibility was often described as immaturity.

Motivation to work

> If someone is motivated to work, there is nothing else that cannot be surmounted. If a young person is not motivated to work, no matter how much support is provided, he/she will fail.
>
> (Worker on a specially designed YTS)

> She didn't want to get on with the work for more than about ten minutes. She would go into the foyer and make long telephone calls to her friend. She didn't care whether the sandwiches were done or not. In the second week they sacked her.
>
> (Pathway Employment Officer)

Chapter 6 shows that the motivation to work of some young people has obviously helped them to succeed, sometimes against great odds.

Ability to relate to colleagues

An ability not to antagonise and upset workmates was seen as important by employers. The positive aspect of relating to colleagues was emphasised by preparation and placement agencies and by young people themselves. It was extended in some instances to include getting along with other employees, employers and supervisors, clients and customers.

'To keep a job you must be able to get on with the people you're working with', said a young man with partial sight and epilepsy. Others interviewed agreed with him.

Ability to get to and from work

Many young people are unable to get a job because they cannot travel independently or organise a means of getting to work. Five specialist careers officers and four Pathway Employment officers, for example listed the ability to travel to work as a crucial factor in determining employability.

Ability to understand and carry out instructions

The ability to do the job and to understand and carry out instructions, at whatever level the job demands, was the most frequently identified competence for employment. Some employers have gone to considerable trouble to find ways of enabling employees, who were unable to read, to follow instructions in pictures or photographs.

Acceptable hygiene and appearance

Poor personal hygiene may make a young person almost impossible to place. If employment is gained, poor basic hygiene can mean losing the job. Young people with learning difficulties and those with a visual impairment may need particular training and support in maintaining an appropriate appearance.

Appropriate social behaviour

Acceptable social behaviour varies to some extent from work place to work place, and it is important that young people can adapt their behaviour accordingly. Behaviour which is acceptable and unremarkable in a segregated setting, such as an Adult Training Centre, may prove to be a barrier to employment.

A 'pleasant' manner

This is obviously a contentious issue, but it was frequently mentioned by the full range of those interviewed. Young people are thought to be more likely to succeed in employment if they have a 'pleasant' personality and are easy to get along with.

'Friendliness', 'willingness to please', 'enthusiasm' and a 'good, happy personality', were mentioned by young people themselves as important factors in getting and keeping a job.

Ability to survive in the world of work

Some resilience and lack of vulnerability is considered to be essential if a young person is going to remain in employment, particularly the kind of resilience which enables the young persona to continue in the face of setbacks. Special schools and specialised adult provision are seen to face difficulties in preparing young people for the realities of the harsher outside world.

> A young man with a visual impairment filled the salt and pepper pots up wrongly in the luncheon club where he was working. When he was asked to empty and refill them he walked out and would not return to work.
>
> (Employer)

Ability to work without total supervision

This was considered to be important but employers were willing to be flexible and supportive in the early days of employment.

I would like them to have some initiative, but it wouldn't matter if they weren't sure of themselves to start with.

(Employer)

Ability to keep work separate from other aspects of life

Some young people with disabilities failed in employment because other aspects of their lives, which are usually kept separate, spilled over into their work environment. They seemed not to have learned to take on different roles for different areas of their lives.

For example, a young woman with learning difficulties would not do any work because she was upset about quarrels with her boyfriend. Although the personnel manager was initially sympathetic, she was told that she must get on with the job.

When she was not able to do this she was eventually given verbal and written warnings and finally lost her job.

Personal autonomy

Many of the comments made by the people interviewed centred on concepts of maturity, independence and an appropriate level of personal autonomy for young people entering employment.

A majority of the preparation agencies see the development of autonomy as central to their work.

This shared perception of the meaning of employability is the basis for an 'employability curriculum' which enables young people to develop the commonly agreed competence that they will be expected to demonstrate.

TVE and CPVE offer routes to competence for some young people. Youth Training Schemes aim to provide an extension of the 'Employability Package' in a work setting which acts as a bridge between education and employment. It is vital that young people with disabilities have access to these initiatives as well as to additional ways of addressing their difficulties.

BARRIERS TO EMPLOYMENT

In response to questions about the factors which make it difficult for young people with disabilities to get a job, replies fell into two major categories:

– those which related to young people themselves;
– those which related to external factors.

Young people who do not have the 'Employability Package'

This was seen as a major barrier to employment. Four examples of responses are given here:

> Principally, lack of understanding about the world of work and employment.

> Many employers are considerate and prepared to make allowances, but faced with rebellious and sullen attitudes by young people who do not appreciate that there may be changes of priority in the work being performed, (i.e. become rigid and resort to job description), they may decide to 'let them go'.
>
> (Manager, Rehabilitation Unit)

> Employees' lack confidence. Lack of social awareness. Mobility fears.
>
> (Young woman who is totally blind)

> Young people sometimes don't understand what work is all about. They don't understand why punctuality and getting on with the job are important.
>
> (Employer)

> Lack of independence; lack of ability to understand what's expected. Behavioural problems or lack of dependability.
>
> (Specialist Careers Officer)

Where young people do not have the 'Employability Package' their difficulties may not have been addressed sufficiently by the preparation process. Some of them may need to leave work and be more effectively prepared, others will need support from employers in achieving the required competence.

YT offers appropriate preparation for work for many learners but is not able to offer support *into* employment when it is often most needed.

Schools and colleges are increasingly focusing their work on employability as part of the transition to adulthood.

Many more courses in further education and some school work are now accredited as part of a progression into the National Vocational Qualification and General National Vocational Qualification frameworks.

This development has two important functions:

– It gives young people with severe learning difficulties access to the same framework for vocational preparation as all other young people.
– It acknowledges a progression to adult status through a preparation for employability for young people with severe learning difficulties.

CHAPTER 7

SELF ADVOCACY

Any effective transition programme must be based on the principles of self advocacy.

Any good programme for transition must be designed to ensure a central role for people who as adults will need to be able to speak for themselves. The transition programme aims at giving young people choice. It gives them a voice which is effective in bringing about change in their own lives.

Further Education Unit document - *Developing Self Advocacy Skills*, (1990), states that the core components of self advocacy are :

– being able to express thoughts and feelings with assertiveness if necessary;

– being able to make choices and decisions;

– having clear knowledge and information about rights;

– being able to make changes.

The challenge for everyone working with young people with severe learning difficulties is how to make self advocacy a reality.

Many parents and members of staff will support young people in learning to express their thoughts and feelings up to the point where those feelings challenge what they, the adults, wish young people to do. The same is true of making choices and decisions. While safe decisions are under consideration, such as tea or coffee, cake or a biscuit, the red jumper or the blue jumper, staff and parents feel happy and confident in promoting choice and decision making skills.

Real self advocacy is essentially about changes in power and status and they are accompanied by significant changes in self concept. Individuals are able to find a new identity as adults. Such changes, however, involve staff and parents letting go of power, and allowing young people to make real choices and decisions. Staff and parents may need considerable support in being enabled to accept a changing balance of power as young people with severe learning difficulties become genuine self advocates.

The following check-list which is adapted from *Developing Self Advocacy Skills with People with Disabilities and Learning Difficulties,* published by The Further Education Unit in 1990 and written by Mariette Clare, may prove useful to practitioners who wish to ensure that self advocacy is effectively included at the core of all learning for adolescents.

A check-list for schools, college courses, or training programmes working with young people with severe learning difficulties

Policy

1. Is there a written commitment to self advocacy in your provision?
2. Is there a genuine assumption that adulthood is the same for people with learning difficulties as it is for the rest of society?

Resources

1. Are there time-tabled opportunities to practice self advocacy activities?
2. Are appropriate videos, teaching material and information packs about self advocacy available?

Staff development

1. Is there in-service training about the principles and practice of self advocacy?
2. Is information about new thinking and new developments routinely circulated to staff in a user friendly way?

Support for Staff

1. Are there regular staff or team meetings?
2. Does management offer active support to staff involved in self advocacy work with young people?
3. Is there an induction period for new staff members?

4. Are team-building exercises regularly undertaken?
5. Do staff feel supported and confident in enabling young people to make real choices and decisions and to effect genuine changes in their lives?

The Environment

1. Do young people have some personal space?
2. Are there opportunities for privacy?
3. Are the decor and furnishings attractive and in keeping with adolescent development?

Regulations

1. Are all the facilities easily available to young people?
2. Are the young people free to move around?
3. Are the young people involved in drawing up any necessary regulations?
4. Are the young people introduced to issues about personal appearance and self-presentation and then given the same choices as other young people - in having their hair and clothes the way they want them?

Sharing Power

1. Is there an independent students' committee or student council?
2. Are its office's members elected by other young people?
3. Is notice taken of the wishes and decisions of the student council?

Programmes Centred on Young People

1. Is there a defined induction programme when people enter the provision for the first time?
2. Are all assessment procedures fully explained to the young person?
3. Are the young people asked about their goals and their needs?
4. Are the young people's opinions recorded?
5. Are all the assessments recorded and the learners given a copy in a format that the young people can understand?
6. Are the young people present at meetings which make decisions about their future?
7. Are all learning activities based on individually identified needs?

8. Is there a written or agreed contract about such programmes?
9. Are the contracts regularly reviewed?
10. Is there a system by which parents and carers can make their views known?

Negotiation and Choice

1. Are young people always consulted about such basic matters as being touched, lifted or being taken somewhere else if they are in a wheel-chair?
2. At the start of a session do staff seek to gain the young peoples' consent to the content and method of teaching?
3. Is it genuinely acceptable for young people to say 'no'?
4. Is it accepted that young people may have legitimate criticisms of a member of staff?
5. Can programmes be changed at a young person's request?
6. Is there always a choice of activities within sessions?
7. Is there alternative provision for young people who want to opt out of a session?
8. Is one to one guidance and counselling available?
9. Are there staff guidelines about when to insist that a young person abides by a contract that he or she has made?
10. Is there a policy of gaining young people's consent to behaviour modification programmes if that is at all possible?

Autonomy

1. Do young people have the opportunity to handle and take responsibility for their own money?
2. Are relationships between young people supported?
3. Do staff sometimes leave young people to resolve their conflicts without interference?
4. Are inter-personal skills fostered and taught?
5. Are young people given the responsibility to get themselves to the right place at the right time with the right equipment?
6. Are young people encouraged to set goals which actually meet their needs?
7. Do staff avoid channelling young people into what they know is available?
8. Do staff support young people in achieving their goals?

Risk Taking

1. Is there an approved set of procedures for staffs to follow when young people are expected to take risks? For example: graded practice, close supervision, consultation.
2. Has management considered and clarified its legal position in this matter?
3. Has management considered how to safeguard both young people and staff against the consequences of accidents?

Evaluation

1. Do the differences between the initial and final assessment by young people and staff indicate positive changes?
2. Do the destinations young people go on to suggest the successful move towards adult status?
3. Can staff and management give clear statements about their aims and objectives in terms of self advocacy?
4. Can staff and management clearly explain how their methods of practice relate to self-advocacy?

To be effective, self advocacy like transition, must be a policy issue with management and staff fully committed to enabling young people to make their vital transition towards autonomy and independence as young adults.

The issues of self-advocacy for young people are slightly different from those for adults, as adolescents still need to have firm boundaries provided by adults. Other issues however, remain the same.

Self advocacy is successful for young people with severe learning difficulties when it provides them with:

– an understanding of choice;
– a feeling of being regarded;
– a better understanding of the world, its possibilities and difficulties;
– a feeling of self worth;
– the development of skills and competencies;
– competence in risk taking;
– a feeling of safety which makes risk taking possible;
– a feeling of confidence ;
– a feeling of being encouraged and supported as they develop towards autonomy.

Young people who experience successful self advocacy are well on the way to achieving full adult status.

CHAPTER 8

WORKING WITH PARENTS

Parents are the constant factor in the lives of most young people as they make their transition from childhood to adulthood.

Young people may change schools, move into further education, go on to training for work, develop new friends and a new concept of themselves. Parents provide the stability which allows their sons and daughters to take the risks which are the basis of learning, but while they provide stability they will also make a transition and revise their view of, and their relationship with, their children.

Adolescents make great demands of their parents. Throughout childhood parents have cared for and protected their children. Their lives may have centred on their children's needs; this is particularly likely to have been true when a child has severe learning difficulties. As the child moves into and through adolescence he needs his parents less and less. Although this is a liberation for parents as they become able to reclaim their own lives and give more attention to their own needs, it is very painful, it hurts not to be needed, and many parents are in fact still needed. They become the sole carers for their adult children.

Parents do not stop being parents because their sons and daughters grow up. Being a parent is a lifelong experience but for most people active parenting, in the sense of day to day care and control, ceases as young people grow up. During the adolescent transition a young person ceases to be a dependent child and moves into adulthood. The challenge for all those who work with young people with learning disabilities is how to help young people become adults even when they will need considerable and sometimes extensive support from their parents because of the nature of their learning disabilities.

Parents have survived a great deal by the time their son or daughter with severe learning difficulties reaches adolescence. There will have been the shock, anger, resentment and pain of the discovery that their child has a severe disability.

There may have been numerous hospital visits, medical interventions and specialist therapies. There will have been all the usual stresses of family life with the additional problems which this particular child's disability presents.

No-one wants their child to be disabled, however much loved a child with a disability may be. Most parents will have had no choice, or chance to prepare themselves for the arrival of a child with severe learning difficulties. They arrive suddenly and unexpectedly, and people who may never previously have had any experience of disability are expected to cope with children whose needs are sometimes far beyond those of other children.

In interviews with a range of parents conducted by Alison Wertheimer for *Self Advocacy and Parent* (FEU 1989) a number of common themes could be identified as relevant to the adolescent transition of young people with severe learning difficulties with which parents need support.

Coming to Terms with Past Events and Experiences

Many parents lives have been dominated by events and experiences about the birth and upbringing of their child with severe learning difficulties. They may have had bad experiences of support services and have felt let down on many occasions. Because of this they feel disinclined to take risks:

> The parent of a child who lost half his leg in a road accident when he was using a respite care service may not, for example, be willing to allow her son, now 18, to be trained to cross roads independently.

> A mother who was told that her daughter would need constant care and supervision, and who has provided that, at great personal cost for sixteen years, will find it difficult to believe that she is being 'over protective'.

> The father of a son who has come home covered in spit may find it hard to accept that his son will be safe in college.

When working with young people in transition it is important that their parents feel safe enough to allow them to take risks. Past events and experiences cannot be taken away but they do sometimes need putting into perspective. Having their knowledge and experience valued may be helpful in achieving this.

Handing over Power and Control

Parents have the power of life and death over all young children. Many parents of adolescent sons and daughters with severe learning difficulties still exercise a considerable degree of control over their lives. For those with profound learning difficulties this power and control may still be at the level it was in babyhood.

Parents often see themselves as the point where the buck stops. When professionals go onto other jobs, or when support services fail, parents retain a feeling of responsibility which makes them reluctant to hand over power and control. A level of independence may be acceptable to some parents where they still retain the real power and control. This is understandable when parents feel they retain responsibility. The concept of an individual with severe learning difficulties taking responsibility in as many areas as possible for him or herself is attractive in theory but it demands real courage to make it a reality.

Independence for Dependent People

Parents whose sons and daughters require considerable physical care have particular difficulties in considering or supporting their independence. The whole household may revolve around an individual's care needs. Parents, particularly mothers, may have made great sacrifices to accommodate a child's dependence and by the time the child reaches adolescence may have built their lives around them. They may now have few other roles in life.

Accepting Individual Privacy and Confidentiality

Young people over the age of 18 may, if they have the capacity to do so, choose to keep any aspect of their life private and confidential from their parents. Teachers, college staff, social workers or residential staff may have to make the decision as to whether a young person has the capacity to make this decision. Parents may disagree with the decision.

Until recently services for people with learning difficulties have seen parents, rather than the people themselves, as the appropriate group to consult with. This is now changing but parents of children with very severe or profound learning difficulties feel they should represent their sons' and daughters' views. Parents may need encouraging to explain the concept of whether they can ever represent their sons' and daughters' interests fully as these may be, as is often the case with all parents of adult children, in conflict with their own interests.

Confronting Risk Taking

Most young people take risks without the knowledge of their parents. Adolescence is a time of extreme risk taking and for a number of young people these are life or death risks and include:

- pregnancy;
- high speed driving;
- drugs;
- dangerous sports;
- dangerous activities such as hitch hiking, adventurous travel or creating a new life with people who are initially strangers.

Almost all young people survive and benefit from risks which would never be accepted by their parents, if they knew about them. The parents of young people with severe learning difficulties are often aware of every risk, or possible risk, to their sons or daughters.

Many young people are so closely supervised that almost all risks, even very minor ones such as burning one's fingers on the oven or nicking one's face shaving, are eliminated. Young people without learning difficulties continually push out the boundaries of risk taking and it would be almost impossible to exert the same degree of protection from risk taking over them.

Parents and staff of all sorts frequently need support in distinguishing between appropriate risks, which should be a normal part of life and being 'at risk', which involves negligence or inappropriate expectations. Decisions about this can only be made on an individual basis on individual occasions but they do have to be made if the lives of young people with learning difficulties are to be as rich and varied as possible.

Developing a Perception of Adult Status

It is hard for all parents to think of their sons and daughters as adults and to treat them as such. Parents of sons and daughters with severe learning difficulties may have particular difficulties because the society in which they live fosters the image of their sons and daughters as perpetual children.

Coming to Terms with Independence and Separation

Most of the proceeding sections can apply to staff as well as parents, but parents alone have to come to terms with the emotional impact of the separation from a much loved child which is a feature of all growing up. Emotional independence from parents is usually considered to be an integral part of the transition to adulthood but it can be very hard for parents to contemplate when they feel a continuing responsibility for their children and may have to provide extensive services for them.

If these are some of the issues for parents facing the transition of a son or daughter with severe learning difficulties into adult life, what will support them in coming to terms with letting go?

The following have been identified by parents as positive ways in which they can be supported:

- *having services available:* many parents are forced into a role of service provider which makes it impossible for them to separate their own lives from those of their children.
- *having parental experience acknowledged and valued.*
- *having professionals who treat parents as equals:* professionals are most frequently criticised for over-controlling and for not really listening.
- *getting support when it is needed:* particularly as an individual in your own right, not just on behalf of your child. Parents need to be seen as legitimate recipients of support for themselves.
- *having access to advice.*
- *having professionals involved who have the right skills for their jobs:* who can be trusted, who are supportive and who can act as facilitators and enablers.

Parents have a crucial role to play in the successful transitions of their sons and daughters into adult life. If a son or daughter has severe learning difficulties the task is a very difficult one. No professional has a right to intervene in family life unless they believe that unlawful activity is taking place, but good professionalism involves enabling people to move on in their thinking.

No-one's rights take precedence. Family life is always a tightrope of negotiation. Young people with severe learning difficulties have the right to adulthood. Parents also have the right to live the life they wish.

Different people should support young people and adults with severe learning difficulties and their parents. Each group has distinctive and separate needs which need to be negotiated.

The critical factor in support is the acknowledgement of separate agendas. A family with young children can be seen as a unit. A family which contains adult children has become a series of linked units. The units do not always have the same needs. Their wishes will certainly be different. Support services must be delivered in ways which acknowledge this difference and legitimise it.

All services which seek to support families must consider the following principals:

1. Any initiatives such as parent support groups need to recognise the individuality of families.
2. Services working with young people with disabilities and with their families should be aware that the wishes and interests of young people and their parents will not always be the same. If at all possible, separate professionals are needed to work with these conflicts if and when they arise.
3. Support offered to parents needs to be continuous and consistent in its approach.
4. Both parents and professionals need to recognise that they may have different views on a range of issues relating to the independency of people with disabilities. Professionals need to understand the reason why parents hold particular views about transition.
5. The parent and the young person are each entitled to privacy and confidentiality and those working in services need to acknowledge and respect that right.
6. Parents are likely to differ in the degree to which they wish to be involved in supporting a young person's move to independence. This should be respected.
7. Parents may wish to obtain advice and support for themselves separately from any services or initiatives relating to the young person and services should recognise that parents may have needs of their own.
8. Support for parents may be particularly welcome at key points in a young person's transition, such as when they are leaving school, leaving home or starting work as these times are likely to be the most stressful and challenging for parents.
9. Support structures for parents should enable them to exercise some choice about how and when the support is offered. Some parents

may prefer to talk to someone on a one to one basis while others may prefer to meet in a group for example.

10. Parents need to feel that they have a positive role to play in supporting the young person's transition to adulthood, and services need to recognise that parents make a positive contribution.

(This list is adapted from *Self Advocacy for Parents,* FEU 1989).

Any agency working with young people in transition must clearly acknowledge that a range of other organisations have a part to play in meeting the needs of parents and of the young people themselves, including health and social services, parent organisations, self advocacy groups and organisations and local and national voluntary organisations.

The contribution of particular agencies and professionals should be based on their particular expertise and experience. For example: national parents' organisations might be involved in disseminating written information and initiating debate on the challenges for parents during transition.

Effective parental support will require sufficient liaison between the various agencies involved, both at the level of individual families and at agency level.

Support for parents needs to start well before the person leaves school and should be available to parents after the young person has made their transition into adult life. A range of strategies will be required for the support of parents and young people and should be developed in response to what people say they would find helpful. Support needs to be offered in ways which parents and young people find useful and acceptable. This will involve considerable interagency collaboration.

CHAPTER 9

INTERAGENCY COLLABORATION

The benefits of agencies working together to provide services to people with disabilities are widely documented and accepted.

This chapter will explore some of the particular issues for support for young people in adolescence.

The Paradox of Support for Adult Status

This book emphasises adolescent transition as a vital stage towards adulthood. Chapter 2 emphasises the support needs of young people. School, further education and youth training schemes offer considerable support to young people as part of their provision and many other agencies such as the career service, social services, voluntary organisations, community learning disability teams also offer a range of support services.

Many people with severe learning difficulties need extensive support from a range of agencies for the whole of their lives. Adult status, on the other hand, demands self-sufficiency, but adults with severe learning difficulties need support to be as self-sufficient as possible.

Many people use this paradox of being dependent on support for independence as grounds for arguing that people with severe disabilities cannot be truly adult and therefore need paternalistic systems to control their lives. Support is often seen as incompatible with adult status and as being inconsistent with autonomy.

People who have disabilities are often concerned about agencies working together. They sometimes find agencies intrusive and controlling and the idea of them working together, and thus providing a monolith of control against which the individual is powerless, is often very unnerving.

Support need not, and indeed should not, dis-empower those who use it. Those who need to use support systems should not feel embarrassed, encouraged to be dependent, overwhelmed or perceive themselves as failing. Support is not incompatible with personal autonomy, self-sufficiency, or full adult status if it is managed in ways which make this possible.

All adults, including those who are regarded as very competent and having high status in our society, use support systems. For example; legal support may be provided by a solicitor, financial support by a banker or administrative support by a secretary. Those who use such support to maintain their professional or personal lives do not regard themselves as less than autonomous. This is because the support systems are controlled by the individual concerned who uses them according to his or her own needs and wishes.

Support services for people with disabilities need to view their services in the same way if they are to enable adults with disabilities to operate as autonomous adults. Individuals should have, as far as possible, the choice of when and how to use support services in exactly the same way as they would with other services used by other adults. If the individual controls the support, rather than being controlled by it, there is no contradiction between the need for support and full autonomous adult status.

Adolescence is the period of time when young people with severe learning difficulties begin to have some understanding of, and begin to learn to take charge of, the systems which will enable them to live their adult lives as independently as possible. Schools and colleges, as establishments which are about learning, have a major role in helping young people to learn to take on this aspect of adulthood as part of the programme of adolescent development. Services have an obligation as well, to ensure that the provisions they make and the structures within which they make them, acknowledge adolescence and adulthood.

The issues for those providing education and training for young people with severe learning difficulties include:

- How to help them understand the support which is available and how to go about using it.
- How to help young people understand something of their own disabilities so that they have some concept of the support they need.
- How to work co-operatively with other agencies on a regular, rather than a crisis basis.
- How to ensure the provision of advocates for young people while they learn how to use support services, or because they have very

severe learning or communication difficulties.

- How to facilitate separate support for parents, if they require it. (This concept of separate support, and the reasons for it, have been discussed in Chapter 7).
- How to keep work with other agencies in perspective. The main aims of schools and colleges for example, are the teaching and learning processes and student achievement.

Interagency work is vital but is also time and energy consuming.

Young people also need to learn how to use agencies effectively to meet their own needs, if they are going to be able to do this in adult life.

To do this successfully, staff must acknowledge that their students need support which is not needed by the general population. They must also feel that they are able to make the students understand this.

Many young people with disabilities are handicapped by a pretence that they are just like everyone else. Whilst it is undoubtedly true that people with learning difficulties or any other disabilities are of equal value to all other members of the community, they are not the same. If they are to have appropriate support this must be acknowledged. Their right to have as much control as possible over that support must also be acknowledged if their adult status is to be supported.

However difficult interagency work may be, it is easier for the agencies to work together *for* individuals with learning difficulties rather than *with* them.

Numerous mechanisms for interagency collaboration have been devised at an individual, local or regional level. Staff from different agencies are trained either separately, or in cross-agency events, to take account of:

- different agency cultures and ways of working;
- different uses of language and terminology;
- different professional areas of expertise;
- different perspectives in understanding the needs of people with learning difficulties, which lead to different methods of service delivery.

Agencies are exhorted to work together and ensure that their individual contributions are co-ordinated and that there are no overlaps or gaps in service provision. They are also encouraged to focus on the individual, to ensure that his or her views are taken into consideration.

Many agencies also encourage the concept of self advocacy, or the inclusion of an individual's advocate in determining services if he or she cannot communicate effectively or cannot conceptualise his or her own needs because of a professional, intellectual impairment.

Many agencies would also feel that it is right and proper that the individual concerned should have at least some degree of control over the services he or she receives. Very little thought has yet been given to how young people with severe learning difficulties learn how to do this.

During adolescence all young people gradually learn to use and direct a number of the services they need as they progress towards adulthood. Elements of the knowledge they need are taught at school or on general education courses at college.

For example:

- opening a bank account;
- securing a mortgage;
- using a family planning clinic;
- renting a flat;
- using a complaints procedure.

Other elements are learned incidentally through family events or individual need.

The families of young people with learning difficulties are unlikely themselves to be using the range of support services that their sons and daughters will be using in adult life. Young people with severe learning difficulties find it difficult to learn incidentally - that is, to learn things just by picking them up rather than being taught.

They do need to be taught how to use an interagency network of support services. The curriculum should therefore address this, if it is to genuinely facilitate an adolescent transition.

Understanding Support and How to Use It

Young people with severe learning difficulties are often taught about the support services which are generally used by the whole population:

- doctors and hospitals;
- dentists;
- the police and fire service;
- public transport;
- communication systems such as the postal service and the telephone system;
- shop staff.

Information about services and how to use them are taught under such headings as 'People Who Help Us' or 'People Whose Jobs Are Important'. The work is often carried out as part of a programme on employment, however, rather than as part of a learning process that would enable the students to make use of the services they need, with as much support as is appropriate.

Schools and colleges rarely discuss the services provided by:

- advocates;
- social workers;
- residential care staff;
- community learning disabilities (or mental handicap) teams;
- voluntary organisations which run services like clubs or daytime activities;
- specialist employment offices;
- day centre staff.

The curriculum does not usually help young people to understand these services, in however rudimentary a way and therefore, does not begin the process of helping the students to use the services in their adult lives.

If schools and colleges are committed to the concepts of adult status and an effective adolescent transition into adulthood, the curriculum on offer should ensure that they begin to provide the information which is needed.

Understanding One's Own Disability

One major difficulty in the introduction of young people to the support services they may use in adulthood is the confrontation of their disability that this entails.

Young people for whom it is at all possible, however, need to have some concept of their own disability for a number of reasons. The main concern of this chapter is the basis for the appropriate use of inter-agency support which such an understanding gives but that is not the only reason for helping young people understand something of their own disability:

- Some young people have very unreal expectations of their own employment prospects - 'I want to be a pilot' or 'I'm going to be a doctor'. When young people with severe learning difficulties make such comments they are often unchallenged and smiled at. If people are patronised in this way and thought of as 'sweet' or 'cute' their dignity is compromised.
- Some young people put themselves at risk because they have not learned about the limitations they have in some areas of functioning. It is unwise, for example, to start out on a new journey if you have a speech problem and cannot effectively tell the bus

driver where you want to go to. Young people need to know if
their speech is unclear to others so that they can learn strategies
which will promote their independence.

If you are disabled and this is kept from you, you are not being treated
with dignity or accorded equal status.

Working with Other Agencies as Routine

Schools, colleges and agencies which prepare young people for employment need to be fully meshed into an interagency network as a matter
of routine if they are to support young people with severe learning
difficulties in using this network effectively.

In some learning situations, for example, students build up a dossier
of useful personal information. Teachers should consider helping students prepare such a dossier of the various support agencies which they
could use, which includes the names of key people, which can be kept
updated and travel with the young person through different provisions
for use in adult life.

The Provision of Advocates

Advocates, by their very nature, are able to function most effectively
and promote an individual's wishes or best interests most satisfactorily
if they are independent of the agencies which provide services.

Educational services are therefore not in a position to provide independent advocates but their major roles could be in:

- pressing for, or helping young people press for, advocates;
- helping those young people who are able to do so learn about and
  use advocates to express their views;
- promoting the view that advocacy can be part of a learning process
  which leads to self advocacy. Advocates can not only represent the
  views of young people, but teach them how to represent their views
  themselves.

Young people who are separating themselves from their childhood
and from the family unit as it was during their childhood, may need to
learn how to advocate for themselves to their parents, or use an
advocate to do this.

This is obviously a very sensitive area, but support for young people
to begin this process is often vital. Teachers must be clear, however,

that the point of the challenge to parent by adolescent is that they take it on themselves. The purpose is defeated if staff challenge parents and keep the individuals themselves in a childlike role. The only person who has the right to challenge parents about his or her gaining adult status is the individual him or herself (or an advocate clearly speaking on his or her behalf). Education can give young people the concepts and the confidence to do this, but educational staff should be wary of taking on the role themselves.

Separate Support for Parents

Many schools and some specially designed college courses offer support to parents as part of their overall work in the area of transition. This can work very well as long as it is clearly separate from work with the young people themselves and the same staff are not involved.

Keeping Interagency Work in Perspective

Every agency has a duty to provide a range of services. That is its major reason for existing. It is very easy however, for interagency collaboration to be so time consuming that the reason for some agencies' existence becomes distorted. Teachers must spend the majority of their time and effort in teaching and the promotion of learning. If the bulk of a staff member's time is being spent in liaison and negotiating with other agencies, and they are not employed as a liaison worker, the balance needs to be redressed. This can be a particular issue for people working with adolescents when a range of children's services may still be involved as well as adult services.

Liaison between school and college, and between college and the next phase of provision is vital and must be systematic and professional. As with all other interagency work, however, a vital learning process in being in control must be developed for as many young people as possible and built explicitly with the curriculum.

Schools and colleges will help young people become successful adults if they help them learn how to take on real adult roles. The adult roles will vary according to individual differences and according to the degree of intellectual disability. No-one can take on an adult role in working with the agencies who service him or her without learning how to do it. The curriculum for transition must provide for this.

CHAPTER 10

AUDIT

Whether you work in school, a college of further education or in an agency which trains young people for work, you will need to operate a quality assurance system to ensure that your work really helps young people with their adolescent transition.

This chapter contains a framework to help you begin this process. You can use it as it is, or adapt it to your own situation. Ideally, you should work on it with all the staff involved with young people between about thirteen and twenty five in your school, college, scheme or centre. A set of forms is provided to guide you.

To be effective in evaluating your work you must be honest, both with yourself and other people. This can be very painful, particularly for staff who are very emotionally committed to their work. You will need to be sensitive in your honesty, without forgetting that you cannot allow bad practices to go unchallenged.

The audit demands that each person looks at their own work and wherever possible individuals also examine each other's work. It demands that the young people have real power to effect change and that they are treated with the beginnings of adult status or dignity. It is aimed at real change.

The audit is in three parts:

– real adolescence
– the curriculum
– pushing the boundaries.

If possible carry it out with at least one other person and record your views and answers.

Real Adolescence

'Real Adolescents don't dust shelves!'

Look at adolescents

This section is to clarify your own knowledge of adolescence and give you a context for your own work.

a) Visit a comparable facility to your own which works with young people who do not have severe learning difficulties. This could be:

–   a secondary school (Year 9 upwards);
–   a sixth form college, if you work with 16 - 19 year olds;
–   a further education course;
–   a Youth Training provision.

If you work on a specially designed course in a further education college, visit another course, perhaps a General National Vocational Qualification course or a GCSE re-take group.

If you work in a day centre with young people, visit a college or Youth Training Scheme but ensure that it does not cater especially for young people with learning difficulties.

Sit in on a session, observe the young people as they arrive, take breaks and relate to adults and to each other. Use the form on page 72 to guide your observations. List all the behaviours which you regard as particularly adolescent and try and work out why the young people concerned behave in that way because they are going through the adult transition.

For example; you may note behaviour which aims to attract the attention of the opposite sex which takes place because of the drive to ultimately establish sexual relationships; or behaviour which challenges adult authority because young people wish to emancipate themselves from it.

Look at the groupings. How do young people relate to each other? Do friendship groups include both young men and women?

Look at clothes, hairstyles and accessories. Which are particularly typical of adolescent and young adulthood? Are there different sub-groups?

Observe the behaviour of adults in the setting and record your observation on Audit Form 1b.

b) Visit a specially designed facility. This could be:

–   a special school or unit;

– a specially designed course for students with severe learning difficulties;
– a specially designed Youth Training provision;
– a day centre for adults with severe learning difficulties.

It could be, of course, the provision where you work, but if you take this option, it is vital that you take on the role of visitor/observer and do not have any active role in what is going on.

Again, look at the behaviour of the young people. List the behaviour which is particularly adolescent. What do the young people do and why do they do it? Use Audit Form 2 to record your observations.

Look at the grouping. How do young people relate to each other and to the adults?

How typically do clothes, hairstyles and accessories reflect adolescence or young adulthood?

Again, observe the behaviour of adults as well and record your observations on Audit Form 2b.

Now use your four completed forms to compare the two settings and begin the evaluation of your own work. Forms 3 - 5 provide a structure for this.

If you think about and analyse your findings honestly you are likely to find that the adolescent experience for young people with learning difficulties is very different from the experiences of their non-disabled peers.

Look at your own work in the light of what you have found.

AUDIT FORM 1

Looking at adolescents

Age of group observed: _____

Setting: _____

Adolescent behaviour

What did they do?	Why?

Groups

What groups formed?	Why?

Clothes, hairstyles, accessories What was adolescent?	What effect did clothes etc create?

AUDIT FORM 1b

Looking at adolescents

Age of group observed: _____

Setting: _____

Adult behaviour

How did those adults present respond to adolescent behaviour?

How did the adults' behaviour differ from the way they would
have responded to children?

AUDIT FORM 2

Looking at adolescents with Severe Learning Difficulties	
Age of group observed: _____	
Setting: _____	

Adolescent behaviour	
What did they do?	Why?

Groups	
What groups formed?	Why?

Clothes, hairstyles, accessories What was adolescent?	What effect did clothes etc create?

AUDIT FORM 2b

Looking at adolescents with Severe Learning Difficulties

Age of group observed: _____

Setting: _____

Adult behaviour

How did those adults present respond to adolescent behaviour?

How did the adults' behaviour differ from the way they would have responded to children?

AUDIT FORM 3

Use the following to score this sheet:

Group without learning difficulties A
Group with learning difficulties   B

Grading 1 - very important or significant
    2 - quite important or significant
    3 - could be important or significant
    4 - of little or no importance or significance
    5 - not observed

How important or significant were the following in the groups you observed?	Group A	Group B
- Adult guidance in an almost equal relationship		
- Challenging/arguing with adults		
- Taking responsibility for oneself		
- Being a potential worker		
- Social activities		
- Friendship groups		
- Sexuality		
- Dress or styles which challenge adults		
- Childhood exemptions or not being responsible for one's own actions		
- Projections into the future eg. "When you leave school......"		
- Conformity to peer group standards		
- Conformity to adult standards		
- Being well behaved		
- Rejection of adult standards		
- Adults being in control		

AUDIT FORM 4

Your own Provisions

For this key piece of work you need to imagine that you are working with young people who do not have severe learning difficulties, but who need to learn very basic things.

Look at the **Physical Environment** where you work.

List the things that adolescents without severe learning difficulties would probably feel uncomfortable with.

Consider:

– the furniture (Do you have infant style trays for example?)
– the wall displays
– the colour scheme

If a complete stranger walked into the room would she think immediately that it was an adolescent/young adult work place?

List the things that adolescents without severe learning difficulties would prefer to have.

Look at the **equipment**

If you were learning the same things as your students, would you be happy for someone you wanted to respect you, to see you using the equipment?

Would non-disabled young people feel happy using it?

Consider the **activities** - the content may be very appropriate, but could it be managed through different activities?

Are you encouraging your students to think of themselves as children by the way you treat them, even while you are talking about 'being grown up'?

Listen carefully to yourself and your colleagues.

Would you use the same tone of voice, vocabulary or rewards with adolescents of the same age who did not have severe learning difficulties?

Do you say 'Good girl' to an 18 year old when 'Well done' or 'Good' would be more appropriate?

Are you **skipping adolescence**?

Most adolescents do not:

- dust
- make sponge cakes or apple pie
- wear "sensible" clothes
- go to bed early
- behave well towards adults
- do what they are told without question
- eat sensibly
- plan carefully
- keep their cupboards, drawers and rooms tidy
- behave in an exemplary way towards the other sex.

Are you expecting young people with severe learning difficulties to move straight from childhood to sensible middle age?

Many young people are frozen in childhood but many are also moved into a premature passive adulthood with too few opportunities to develop an individual adult identity which is different from the wishes of parents and teachers.

What did you find?

AUDIT FORM 5

The Curriculum

Does what you teach and how you teach it give adolescents real power and control?

The role of the Curriculum in Empowerment

The total learning experience empowers if:

- the content of the curriculum meets the learners' needs as they are now. Are you teaching the most important things?
- the process of the curriculum (how, where, etc, the content is taught) enables the learner to make sense of what he/she is learning. How do you think that? Do they know why they do things?
- the timetable makes sense. How do elements relate to each other?
- the ethos of the establishment is supportive and facilitating of challenge. If a student argues can he ever win?
- advocacy is encouraged and valued. Do you *really* listen to parents or other advocates?
- self-advocacy skills are made explicit in the curriculum and are taught so that young people learn to have views and to express them.
- individuals are realistically valued, not sentimentalised.
- involvement of the learner is basic to decision making at whatever level he or she can participate.
- self evaluation is taught to all young people. Records for Achievement can be valuable tools.
- there is a whole service policy on empowerment which is delivered in practice. This is a very challenging idea!

AUDIT FORM 6

Measure of Quality

- Is the work taking place in a real adolescent environment?
- Are appropriate aids and equipment used?
- Are adolescent privacy and dignity respected?
- Are learning needs reviewed?
- Is technology reviewed?
- Do real choices exist? Are they made available by staff?
- Are experiences of integration available?
- Are parents appropriately involved?
- Is learning seen as a *contract* between professionals and the young person?
- Is there a commitment to, and arrangements for self advocacy?

AUDIT FORM 7

Thoughts and Questions

Remember:

- We often think we are promoting adolescence when we are not. An inspector once observed a lesson about independent cookery where the students were not allowed to turn on the cookers. No matter how much independence is given to young people with severe learning difficulties, someone else often holds the key element!
- Put in as much support as someone actually needs - not how much you need to allay your fears. Risk taking and risk management should be part of any policy document for adolescents and all staff should be informed and trained to deliver the policy.
- Adolescence is not the same in all cultures although the tasks remain the same everywhere. Discuss the issues with parents and members of different religious and cultural groups so that your provision is sensitive to different concepts of adult status and dignity.
- Enabling young people with severe learning difficulties to become more genuinely adolescent will promote conflict at home and wherever you work. It is hard to accept that goodness, passivity, sensible behaviour and conformity should be challenged.

How will you:

- ensure that your provisions genuinely promote adolescence and challenge practice which does not?
- ensure that a risk taking and risk management policy is in place and it is used? How will you support parents and staff in allowing students to make mistakes and take risks as they learn?
- make the adolescent experience appropriate for young people from different cultural and religious backgrounds?
- manage opposition to the emerging adolescent behaviour which causes more problems than the existing unquestioning conformity?
- push young people into adolescence when it is safer and more comfortable to be a child who is looked after and does not have to take any responsibility or stand by views or decisions?

AUDIT FORM 8

Write a summary of your findings for presentation to management and staff.

You will need to consider the following:

- How will you portray the importance of a proper adolescent transition?
- What **strengths** does your provision already have?
- What **weaknesses** need to be addressed?
- Why?
- What are you actually asking people to do?
- How will you involve the young people?

AUDIT FORM 9

Devise an action plan together:

It should have:

- realistic targets
- dates and strategies for achieving them
- individual named areas of responsibility
- a built-in review process
- interagency, parental and student involvement
  for the best chance of success.

AUDIT FORM 10

Keep a record of changes and improvements

If you do not record you will not be able to celebrate
success or challenge failure.

The curriculum cycle applies to this as to all other
work.

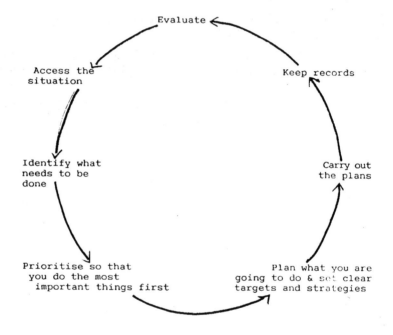

SELECTED BIBLIOGRAPHY

Aspects of Adulthood: Sex Education in Further Education for Learners with Severe Learning Difficulties. FEU 1992.

Enabled to Work: Support into Employment for Young People with Disabilities. FEU 1989.

Learning Support for Young People in Transition; Leaving School for Further Education and Work. McGinty and Fish. OU Press 1992.

Developing Self Advocacy Skills with People with Disabilities and Learning Difficulties. FEU 1990.

Adults with Learning Difficulties: Education for Choice and Empowerment. Jeannie Sutcliffe. OU Press 1990.

A New Life. Transition Learning Programmes for People with Severe Learning Difficulties who are Moving from Long-Stay Hospitals into the Community. FEU. 1992.

Young People with Handicaps: The Road to Adulthood. OECD/CERI. 1986.

Obstacles to Work for All. OECD/CERI. 1983.

Index